The BAD MOTHER'S REVENGE

The BaD MOTHeR'S ReVeNGe

a HuMOROUS GUIDe ABOUT COPING (AND SOMeTIMeS NOT) WiTh The JOys OF PaReNTING

SONIA NeALe

ABC
Books

Published by ABC Books for the
AUSTRALIAN BROADCASTING CORPORATION
GPO Box 9994 Sydney NSW 2001

First published in April 2006

The National Library of Australia Cataloguing-in-Publication entry

Neale, Sonia,
The bad mother's revenge : a humourous guide about coping
(and sometimes not) with the joys of parenting.

ISBN 0 7333 1834 7.

1. Motherhood – Humor. 2. Mother and child – Humor.
I. Australian Broadcasting Corporation. II. Title.

306.8743

Cover and internal design by Luke Causby, Blue Cork Design
Typeset in 11 on 16pt Bembo by Kirby Jones
Printed and bound in Australia by Griffin Press

5 4 3 2 1

Acknowledgements

Thanks to the following people.

My husband Dave, for his unwavering support and help over the past twenty years.

My children, who deserve a special mention. Without them, of course, this book would not be possible. To Melissa, Matthew and Christopher, I love you dearly with all my heart, except when you leave wet towels on your bedroom floor and scatter Cornflakes all over the kitchen bench.

My parents, for always being there for me, and my sister Sarah, who has always believed in me and my writing.

Stephanie Calman, creator and editor of the BadMothers Club.co.uk for publishing my very first article on her website and giving me the confidence to believe in myself.

Rosemary Greenham, senior producer, *Saturday Breakfast*, 720 ABC Perth, for her complete faith in me as a Bad Mother and for giving me a radio slot on the basis of an unreturned phone call and a single email.

Sarah Knight, presenter, and Marshall Martin, producer, of *Saturday Breakfast* for their wisdom and encouragement.

Jenny, my therapist, for going above and beyond the call of duty and being very supportive under difficult circumstances.

All my friends with whom I've enjoyed ladies lunches: Jeanette, MaryAnne, Vicki (deceased), Mayette, Maria, Doreen and Christine.

Martha, who, over many a long boozy lunch that turned into many a long boozy dinner, always validated my experiences as a Bad Mother.

Kathryn, who always made me laugh long and hard at the absurdities of life and motherhood.

And last but not least, Yvonne, my childhood schoolfriend who I have shared many dreams and adventures with — and still do.

Foreword

There's something about a teenage daughter. Her photographic memory can retain every nuance of the convoluted plot of her favourite soapie. Her analytical brain can dissect character motivations and likely dramatic developments. But can she take an accurate phone message? Nah. It was one such wrongly taken phone message that brought Bad Mother Sonia Neale into my life.

My first contact with Sonia was an email I received from a woman, a stranger to me at the time, whose daughter had told her that a radio station had phoned. Was it by any chance, the emailer enquired, me at 720 ABC in Perth? It wasn't, but her email about the trials of one family sharing a phone made me laugh out loud, a rare and welcome event on a working Monday morning. And so it was, from this initial email, that a friendship and a radio spot were born.

There followed two years of wonderful, honest, funny radio segments and now this book, which will resonate with anyone who has ever been, or who has had, a mother. It has been a time filled with shared stories of the sane and insane consequences of motherhood.

Our children know that mothers are far from perfect, for which we do not thank the advertising and film industries, which rarely show the lowdowndirty side of family life. But mothers know that there is no halo delivered after the placenta. Or, if there is, mine got lost, probably somewhere under the massive mountain of laundry waiting in vain for some attention to be paid to it.

No, we mothers remain the same funny and flawed creatures we were before we gave birth. We are capable of many low acts: slipping the boring, boring Thomas the Tank Engine book surreptitiously into the log fire after one reading too many (yes, I have done that), the kids put to bed in their school uniforms to save time in the morning (not yet inflicted, but kept in mind as an emergency strategy), the hissed instruction not to tell friends that the reason they have to get off the phone at 9.30 at night is because mum has finally served dinner (happens every night).

Not that it's a one-way street. There is such a thing as the kids' revenge.

Such as the penetratingly clear voice of the 3-year-old child in the supermarket queue, urging me to look at the size of that woman's bottom — 'How *big* must her toilet be?' A few years later (quite a few) the same daughter is now studying beauty therapy. I get to interrupt my working day to be the guinea pig in her waxing exam. Mother–daughter bonding over my bikini line was never mentioned in any parenting manual that I ever read.

It's precious moments such as these that Sonia observes from her own life and the lives of her own family members and preserves for those who follow, thereby providing them with evidence of the real truth of parenting.

Relish this product of Sonia Neale's creative mind. It has taken the family, its love and loyalty, its cunning and ruthlessness, and turned life into tales we can all recognise as the outrageous and heartening behaviour of our own families. It's all about love and survival — the best of both that we can manage.

Read, and recognise yourselves.

By the way, I sometimes wonder who did ring Sonia in the first place and if she is still waiting for her to return the call.

Rosemary Greenham
Senior Producer
720 ABC, Perth

P.S.
My second daughter has just read this foreword and assures me that it's all yuck. Situation normal, then.

Contents

Chapter 4

Q: Are you a fisherwoman or a golf addict?

A: Putting the 'Fun' Back into Dysfunctional

• **69** •

Chapter 5

Q: Teachers. Heroes or villains?

A: Schooldaze, Holidaze, Confused and Dazed

• **87** •

Chapter 6

Q: Why is it so hard to save money?

A: Debtors' Homes and Gardens

• **107** •

Chapter 7

Q: Do you ever feel as though you are faking your life?

A: Guilt Magnets-R-Us

• **125** •

Chapter 8

Q: Why do I get such pleasurable feelings from
chronic self-indulgence?

A: Seven Deadly Sins

• **137** •

Chapter 9

Q: How well can you cook things up?

A: The Four Fs – Fatness, Fitness, Food and Fashion

• 153 •

Chapter 10

Q: Who peels at your house?

A: Therapeutically Speaking

• 165 •

Chapter 11

Q: Shouldn't children look after their parents more?

A: Secret Girls' Stuff

• 191 •

Chapter 12

Q: Why didn't someone teach me this at school?

A: What I have learnt in life

• 217 •

The BAD MOTHER'S REVENGE

1

Q: So, do you want to know what it's Really like?

A: Fornication, Gestation, Lactation, Frustration, Vexation

In the Beginning

'You're pregnant!' said my doctor, fifteen years ago.

Immediately, I sank into a state of blissful consciousness — a state of mind Supreme Buddhist monks spend six months of deep meditation and extreme fasting to achieve.

And there was more bliss to come — much more.

It wasn't until I threw up my breakfast of olives and salami on toast every morning that I truly knew what cravings and morning sickness was all about. Just looking at my toothbrush guaranteed an extra blissful heave.

A pre-paid, pre-pregnant holiday to Bali left me feeling queasy; every morning I hung over the toilet bowl in our Legian Hotel. Not so different from when I'd been to Bali before, in a non-pregnant state, when I somehow always found myself listlessly resting my chin on the rim of the toilet seat, heaving my guts out in exactly the same fashion. Nothing to do with the pub crawl the previous evening of course, and everything to do with drinking the local water.

That's my story and I'm sticking to it.

When we got back from Bali, my boss informed me that day-dreaming about impending motherhood was not in my job description, so I had to give up paid employment.

By this time I had a preggy brain, a state of mind that remains with some mothers until the last child leaves home. I spent the next six months rocking in my armchair, eating for two and watching my kneecaps slowly disappear.

I had no qualms about giving birth. I was having a drug-free, natural birth. Just how hard can it be to breathe and push?

Confidence is a state of mind, never more so than when you are completely ignorant of the facts.

And I was still as ignorant after attending ante-natal classes as I had been when I first walked into the class. Giving birth, I truly believed, would be a series of mildly uncomfortable contractions followed by a slight burning sensation when the baby's head crowned.

These little pearls of wisdom were – of course – written by a man who would never have had the pleasure of delivering something the size of a bowling ball from an orifice the size of a ping-pong ball. If men had to give birth there would be only one child per family. Eventually, not only would we have zero population growth, but we'd also end up with population zero.

The mirth of birth

Having a birth plan is not quite the same as giving birth.

I planned my pregnancy according to the books and glossy magazines I read. Trouble was, my pregnancy hadn't read the same books as I.

I was sixteen days overdue, had gestational diabetes, varicose veins and a haemorrhoid the size of a maternity hospital before high blood pressure dictated I be induced. Postnatal depression put in an appearance even before my baby was born.

In other words, prior to giving birth I felt I had already failed as a mother.

Failure #1: The induction

An induced twelve hour labour, an alarming dose of pre-eclampsia and an epidural that didn't deliver what the glossy magazines had promised it would had not been part of my birth plans.

Pain was never an option. In fact, pain was not an option in any event of my life. Breathing exercises were highly overrated. Besides, should pain occur, the drugs and the spinal tap were going to take care of that particular problem.

Finally, I came to the conclusion that a birth plan, as with a hospital bowel management plan, was yet another of life's oxymorons. No amount of laxatives or enemas can ever prepare you for that first excruciating crap.

If your baby rips you a new vagina then the first post-delivery bowel motion is akin to ripping you a new anus.

Failure #2: My unbreakable waters

OK, so it was a teaching hospital and we had let our medical insurance lapse so we could afford a new nursery. But now, with hindsight, I can see that paying a hefty monthly fee for insurance would have been far less painful than having a medical student spending sixty minutes up my whatsit trying to break my waters.

Finally, the senior doctor came in, put an evil looking hook on his finger, slashed at my vagina once and opened the floodgates.

Failure #3: The epidural

Another real doctor stabbed me in the back with a sharp needle; my husband experienced sympathy pains and promptly passed out. I lay there in agony while the doctors and nurses fussed around, handing him cups of tea and sympathy.

I couldn't wait for him to come around so I could dig my fingernails into his hands during the next contraction, which would have been his punishment for having the effrontery to faint.

Failure #4: The failed epidural (the 'It Could Only Happen to Me' syndrome)

Before the induction started working I was bright-eyed and bushy-tailed, laughing and joking with the staff, thinking that waves of intermittent contractions were, as my mother told me, like riding waves at the beach.

As a teenager I'd suffered badly from period cramps, so I was the full bottle on what to expect, how to expect it and how much to expect.

At last, all lights were green and things were beginning to happen. We'd been fed and watered and excitedly awaited that first contraction. Ten minutes later, when I threw up my dinner and screamed for an epidural, several polar bears at the North Pole put their paws over their ears.

Like thousands of women before me, whose own mothers had subscribed to some conspiracy theory that giving birth was more like a gentle breeze than a fully fledged hurricane, I decided to regress into my childhood and started swearing and crying.

It's my birth and I'll cry if I want to. So I'm a baby giving birth to a baby. What amazes me is that I endured a full ten minutes of unendurable pain before screaming blue murder for the epidural.

It's not that I'm a wimp, it's just that my experience was the most harrowing and torturous ever. In the entire hospital. On the entire continent. In fact, in the whole world.

It was two hours after the epidural was administered before the doctor arrived and yet another two before it started to work. Then the needle began to worm its way out. Another two hours later it fell out. For good.

We learnt our lesson. Next time around we pre-booked the epidural at about the same time I went off the pill. Just to make sure.

I started to point out to the midwife that this wasn't the birth I'd planned, that I was feeling rather cheated. She gave me a mask to suck on. I sucked and sucked, like a baby on its mother's breast. Throughout the night I refused to be weaned and eventually, a tug of war broke out. The nurse, being much cleverer than me, switched the gas from nitrous oxide to oxygen. Without my permission, I might add. I still have issues over that.

And I still have lingering embarrassment over defecating on the labour room table, even though the mess was discreetly removed by a tactful nurse. The things we go through so we can be abused by our children when they become teenagers.

Failure #5: Post-epidural headache

Far worse than any self-induced hangover is the post-epidural headache, the one that makes you want to throw up every time you sit up. I had to sit up a lot in a vain attempt to breastfeed my mostly uncooperative baby.

My head felt brain-damaged and my mutilated nipples were pillars of agony. All my nighties smelled like a yoghurt factory. As well, my breath stank of onions and garlic, even though I hadn't eaten any of these offending vegetables in recent days.

Every person I'd ever known decided to visit at exactly the same time, and they were all in a very jolly and happy mood.

Failure #6: Unnatural childbirth

Years later, after I'd unsuccessfully given birth to my three happy and healthy children, I received a phone call from a very smug first-time mother who proudly told me she'd very successfully delivered the perfect birth plan. I'm not sure if there was a child involved or not. Naturally, her plan was without drugs. Naturally, without pain. Naturally.

Apparently my birth experiences sat somewhere between the abnormal and the artificial. I told her that it's easy for people without feelings to have a pain-free birth.

Failure #7: It's a girl

Somewhere along the line, I got it into my thick head that having a girl first would be a disappointment.

Perhaps I would have been right if I lived in India or China, but Australia is, most of the time, a far more enlightened country.

After a couple of hours I changed my mind and was glad I had a daughter, a view I held on to until she became a teenager.

Giving birth is like getting swept out to sea during a Force 10 hurricane and being repeatedly hit by an ocean liner, until finally, you get tossed into the eye of the storm, only giving birth is considerably more terrifying and painful. Surviving the distance through to the other side is called Parenting.

Multiple climaxes

A euphoric state of intoxicating bliss enraptured with the sheer joy of life itself. This is the definition of my first pregnancy.

Thirteen years later my euphoric state of intoxicating bliss turned into The Exorcist.

Here's some Bad Mother maternity definitions that don't exist in parenting propaganda magazines.

The pregnancy test

This is the acid test designed to undermine even the strongest of relationships.

A pregnant pause

The length of time between a stranger asking, 'When is your baby due?' and your reply that you are NOT. ACTUALLY. PREGNANT.

Here's some wise advice from someone who learnt the hard way. Unless you actually see a baby's head emerging from between someone's legs – never, ever enquire if they are expecting a visit from the stork.

A postnatal examination

This involves having your head examined by a health professional at the very thought of going through pregnancy and childbirth again, with the added bonus of now having a gorgeous little toddler to help you maintain moments of decentralisation as you cognitively regress through the next nine months.

Moments such as these.

Morning sickness

A malady of unknown origin suffered mainly by non-pregnant people who have no desire to get up in the mornings and go to work.

Everything you wanted to know about labour but were afraid to ask

Sheila Kitzinger, Earth Mother Extraordinaire, equates labour and childbirth to riding waves of ecstasy before budding flowers open to full bloom. I read her books before I gave birth to The Exorcist; this line is a classic from Sheila's book.

'Childbirth is like having one huge climactic experience.'

Thank goodness I was not having twins or triplets. I don't think I could have handled multiple climactic experiences.

Without passing judgement, I think Sheila might be faking her childbirths. And why not? After all, I've done a pretty good job of faking motherhood so far.

I was more than two weeks overdue with my daughter and she was dragged out of me by her head, kicking and screaming.

Nothing has changed. I do the same thing every school morning.

My first son not only arrived on schedule, but he also took only five gentle and peaceful hours to do so, thanks to the pre-booked epidural.

With my third child I opted for an elective caesarian, which is why he has a round head and my other two children don't. He weighed 5.5 kilograms.

If I start getting clucky again, I'll be opting for an elective frontal lobotomy.

Bad mother's revenge frictionary - definitions of maternity

Afterpains
The rest of your natural life. Get over it.

Amneurotic fluid
What gets into your bloodstream and makes you cry at anything, even Bruce Willis films.

Anti-natal
Someone who never wants children, not in any circumstances.

Bladdered
The condition we end up in after celebrating the brief moment when all three children attend the same school, in the same location, at the same time.

Co-lick-ed

Finally, coming to the end of that stage where the baby screams and throws up during every feed.

Defoetus

The way we feel, ten years after giving birth to our last child, when we finally admit that motherhood, glittering career and that mature-age university degree just ain't gonna happen.

Delivery sweets

Your wonderful friends who know that Lindt chocolates are better than a basket full of nappy pins, plastic pants and baby bum creams.

Demand feeding

What the rest of the family do if you're dumb enough to let them see you anywhere near the kitchen.

Dumbrella

Taking the baby out in the pram and not noticing the increasingly dark cloud cover. Only when it buckets down do you realise you have left a rather vital piece of equipment back at the house.

Easy-peasy-otomy

Being convinced by virginal hospital staff that a 20 centimetre perineal cut heals quicker than a 2.5 centimetre tear.

Expectant father

Arguably, the most useless piece of equipment in a labour ward.

Fall-open tubes

Where the ova slide down the chute in order to become little people and, eventually, quite big ones who want to borrow the car and stay out all night.

Formulark

Trying to count and pour six scoops of powdered milk into a bottle of boiling water, getting up to number three and wondering if you weren't actually at number four instead, thus having to ditch the whole lot and start the process again. This time you manage to get to number four before you lose count.

Functioning brain

An urban legend.

Home confinement

The next twenty years of your life.

Hormoanal

What he can hear ringing in his ears as he drives down the road.

Hysterectummy

Of course you can't see the scar; your stomach's hanging over it.

La-boring

The thirty-ninth week of your first pregnancy, when you think you are going to die of boredom, not realising that this is actually the best week of your life.

Lack-tation

Having to put baby on the bottle.

Materminator

Threatening your children with bodily harm on a daily basis.

Maternitty gritty

Tall stories and urban legends of the horrors of childbirth.

Menstrual cycle

What your husband gets on to pedal away from the fallout.

Midwiffy

That embarrassing moment during labour when you realise that your intense pushing has produced something other than a newborn healthy baby.

Monopause

The monotony of suffering various indignities due to the ageing process.

Mucus plug

Something left on the floor of the shower after your two boys have been there.

Nazi Nursing Mothers' Association

'We have ways of making you breastfeed.' The NNMA *Manifesto* clearly states that every mother can breastfeed, and if you can't, you just aren't trying hard enough.

Neonatal

A character from *The Matrix*.

Ovary-ters Anonymous

Where hysterectummies go to get in touch with their inner Kate Moss.

Pelvic flawed muscles

Another urban legend.

Placentred

Placid and centred parents who plan on either frying the afterbirth with some broccoli and eating it while imbibing a nice bottle of chianti, or digging it into the soil around their favourite rosebush.

Poo-berty

When your sweet little children morph into insufferable big shits after the hormoanals kick in.

Postnatal check-up

Having your head examined when you start to think about going through all that again.

Postpartum bowel management

An oxymoron.

Sex

Yet another urban legend.

Short-term memorandum

The art of list writing, because you now have the attention span of a Formulark.

Sleeping like a baby

Waking up every two hours after shitting the bed, and then screaming for attention.

Sterilising unit

Equipment you only ever used for the first baby.

Ultrasound asleep

Tiptoeing around the house so as not to wake Princess Precious from her afternoon nap.

Uncontrolled crying

What mothers do on a regular basis.

Utes-R-Us

An Aussie car yard specialising in blue heeler approved utility trucks.

When the milk of human kindness turns to sour cream

Breastfeeding, unlike Robbie Williams's bum, is not all it's cracked up to be. Anyone who has suffered the toe-curling experience of breastfeeding with sore, cracked, scabbed and bleeding nipples, will understand when I say I once broke the footrest off a rocking chair with my foot while breastfeeding my four-day-old, dearly wanted and treasured baby daughter.

Babies have a stronger suck than two engines of a Boeing 747. And believe me, that is something else I do not want to stick my tits into.

And what about afterpains? No, not the ones that last for the next eighteen years. I mean the pains that occur when a hormone is released from what is left of your brain and the milk letdown process begins. This hormone also stimulates your uterus to contract back to its pre-pregnant shape. However, as we all know, when air is released from a balloon, it never quite regains its previous shape.

So not only are your nipples excruciatingly mangled every one to four hours, but your uterus, obviously feeling its heyday is over, also now gleefully starts contracting in time to the baby's suck — and your screams.

I get thoroughly fed up looking at glossy mother and baby magazines and seeing serene mothers feeding angelic babies.

In the glossy magazine pictures that are my life, a frumpy dressing gown-clad mum is holding back acres of flesh-coloured jelly with one hand — two fingers prised open to allow a swollen recalcitrant nipple to protrude up and out — and trying to get the other to connect to a red-faced, screaming watermelon.

It's high time the military maternity machos brought motherhood into the age of reality television, depicting the average mother of a baby and two grubby toddlers.

Let's watch resentful real mum scrape and scrub the scullery to panic-attack perfection and Hoover the unlimited Lego off the lino while 'elegantly breastfeeding a serene, angelic newborn baby'.

Just as doting dad walks through the door, desperately wanting to dump his day onto someone else.

Bugger the housework. I needed two hands just to keep my daughter from getting smothered by my bosoms.

I would watch other mums at playgroup snap open their lycra maternity bras, flash beautifully sculpted breasts, wave baby in the general direction and attach with military precision.

Then, just when I thought things couldn't get any worse, I was told I had inverted nipples. 'They are *not* inverted,' I said, 'they are just too damn scared to come out.'

That's when I ended up with mastitis – which is when the milk of human kindness turns to sour cream – and I finally realised: breastfeeding well and truly sucked.

It was time to turn to the bottle.

White. Dry. Chilled to perfection.

Lifestyles of the tricked and brainless

You've finally given birth. You think you've delivered 3.6 kilograms of pink genetic material, but what you've actually delivered is a completely new lifestyle.

Congratulations! It's a ploy

In the bloom of first pregnancy you smugly tell yourself – and everyone else around you – 'This baby is going to have to fit in with our lifestyle.'

You are having a natural birth because you've read all the pregnancy propaganda books that gently explained, 'When the baby's head tears the perineum, you will feel a slight burning sensation.'

Naturally, you will be breastfeeding your naturally born baby, just as Mother Nature intended because 'Every woman can breastfeed. It's only natural.'

You perform energy-enhancing yoga exercises and do meditation in your immaculate feng-shui approved garden, thus ensuring correct karma for yourself and your growing tummy.

Conversations with your loving spouse will have

- a beginning
- a middle
- an end.

Your hairdresser maintains and nurtures your foiled and blow-waved ego and, during a recent weekend in Fiji, you were charged excess baggage on your make-up case alone.

Your mother takes you out to lunch at a fancy restaurant. Together you solve all the problems of achieving world peace – and she picks up the bill.

At night you sauté, sear and simmer sumptuous cuisine – and care and share the day with your attentive partner.

During the birth of your fourth child you threaten legal action if the hospital doesn't pump you full of drugs. Artificial feeding suddenly became natural when your first baby was six weeks old.

Eight hours sleep is but a vague and distant memory – or it would be if you had any memory left.

Then, your husband nudges you in the back and says, 'Are you awake, hon?'

Your mother arrives for a lunchtime sandwich and, when she gives you constructive advice on maximising household efficiency, your migraine mutates into a brain tumour.

You struggle into a pair of faded leggings and a baggy T-shirt, drive down to the local gym and, without conviction, convince yourself you are not acting on impulse as you sign up and pay for a twelve month non-refundable membership.

Upon star jumping you suddenly realise postnatal exercises were not overrated after all. A year later, you realise they were the single most expensive aerobics lessons in history.

The hairdresser is now just a shop you pass by on your way to another shop where you're going to get a birthday present for someone else's child. Make-up is what you and your husband do on a regular basis.

You all eat in front of the television with *The Simpsons* blaring so loudly that you don't have to talk to each other.

But at least the children have fitted in with your lifestyle.

Sex and the nitty gritty

There comes a time in every parent's life when they have to explain the wondrous intricacies of that short subject, 'The Meaning of Life,' more commonly known as 'The Birds and the Bees', preferably before the children hear strange sounds coming from their parents' bedroom at night.

I was reading a seemingly innocent book about whales to my seven-year-old son. A conversation followed that went like this.

'Why is that whale jumping out of the water?'

'To impress the female whales.'

'Why would he want to do that?'

'So that he can have sex with them.'

'Why do they want to have, umm, sex?' he squeaked, crimson colour appearing on his cheeks.

'So they can have babies.'

I went on to explain in graphic detail just exactly how the birds chirped and the bees buzzed and, just to give him further nightmares, I added, 'That's how you were born!'

'Can I go and help Daddy with the dishes now!' he said, running full pelt out of the room. If I'd known that that was the way to get them doing the housework, I'd have started sooner.

My mother made my cheeks turn crimson, too, many years before when a friend's goat was giving birth and Mum decided it was a great opportunity to get back at me for all the embarrassments I had ever caused her. Pretty much the same reasons I gave all my children the gorier facts of life – to watch them squirm and wriggle and see just how long they could last without actually throwing up.

However, Mum only got as far as 'Let's have a mother and daughter talk about what happened tonight.'

At that point, I faked a tummy ache and stayed in the bathroom for the next three weeks until she gave up.

I dread the stage when three sets of raging teenage hormones pervade our household. I tell my children that my second son was the only child I ever gave birth to with my legs crossed (he was a caesarean) so now we *can* all participate in oral sex around the dinner table.

Talking about it deflates the myths and, as with alcohol and drugs, when the myths are demystified, they are no longer as desirable and the children are less likely to indulge in rampant, casual sex after imbibing loads of drugs and alcohol.

We wouldn't be able to stand it if they had more fun than us.

2

Q: HOW MANY EMOTIONALLY NEEDY CREATURES DO YOU REALLY NEED IN YOUR house?

A: Small Child, Headache; Big Child, Heartache

Emotion in motion

Parenting – the most important thing you will ever stuff up in your life.

I vowed never to make the same mistakes my parents did. And I didn't. I managed to make completely different ones.

My mother admitted to me recently that she made all the mistakes under the sun with me. I said, 'Could I have it in writing, please?'

Kids are hard work. Physically when they are younger, psychologically and emotionally when they are teenagers. I have the grey hairs to prove it, and not just on my head either.

Being a teenager is even more psychologically and emotionally exhausting. I was one of those girls who used to overeat her feelings; life as a size 22 was not much fun. At school it was a case of survival of the fattest.

Girls are hard-wired to punch out each other's emotions; boys just punch out each other's lights and get over it.

My children are not the only emotionally needy critters in our house. Whenever I go to the kitchen, the cats and dog follow me in and the goldfish swim up to the side of the tank where I'm standing, looking hopeful for some nourishment, even if they've just been fed. I had to let my pot plants die over summer because they were becoming just too emotionally needy.

Then my husband gets home in the evening wanting to tell me all about his day at the office. I've learnt to zone out and say 'Hmmm!' and 'Really?' in all the right places.

My emotional neediness gets taken care of at a girls' lunch out – which can sometimes end at 3 o'clock in the morning in a taxi and my head hanging out of the window – and a very worried-looking taxi driver.

The trouble with being a Bad Mother is that my teenage daughter tells me everything, and I mean everything. I listen with wisdom and compassion, and then go to the bedroom and scream into my pillow. But I work as a team – with all the other voices in my head.

Between bites of deep-fried pizza, my daughter's boyfriend advised me against watching the movie *Thirteen* starring Holly Hunter, but, like any rebellious parent, I sat with them and watched it anyway. He said it was rated NRP – Not Recommended for Parents. I hate to say it, but he was right.

I would have had less nightmares watching the director's cut of *The Exorcist*.

All fired up

Sometimes we mothers are blissfully unaware of the dramas that unfold behind our backs in our own household. Sometimes, we just don't want to know.

Such was the case when my two boys regressed to a primitive state and discovered fire, spending one Saturday afternoon very quietly and very productively setting fire to our back garden.

I was reading a good book and pretended they were doing something educational, something constructive. But constructiveness and productivity are not necessarily the same thing. Unbeknown to me, they had stockpiled a considerable stash of weapons of mass destruction, the likes of which Saddam Hussein would have been proud of. The only thing missing was the Semtex. George Bush had been looking in the wrong place. If he'd come into our back garden that day he would still have some credibility as a world leader.

Confronting my two boys with the pile of evidence, I tried to explain about the dangers of fire. In their eyes, of course, I was just being a damp squib.

Boys light fires . . . duh!

So we embarked on a journey to extinguish their pyromaniac tendencies from their systems. We let them light fire after fire. They were even allowed to fire up the barbecue, a very important job usually reserved for dads only. They even fought over who was going to light up my cigarettes.

It took a while, but after about a year they felt they were able to pass by a box of matches without feeling the need to set fire to the whole countryside.

Attraction to dangerous pastimes is universal – girls light fires too. I had gotten in touch with my inner firebug at about the same age as my boys had theirs. In fact, my friend and I often reminisce about lighting our first match, smoking our first cigarette, setting fire to the local bushland and how our backsides burnt when we got caught. We hadn't intended to set it alight, it just got completely out of control, a bit like my entire childhood.

Like the out of control likely lads who set fire to our local bushland every few weeks or so, I have to remember they are not potential arsonists, they are simply experiencing a rite of passage – a bit like shoplifting, wagging school or spraying graffiti on expensive brick walls.

I'm just grateful my boys haven't yet discovered that they can light up their own backside emissions in that time-honoured blokey tradition known as 'Blue Flames.'

Life is like your teenage daughter

According to Forrest Gump, life is like a box of chocolates; you never know what you're gonna get. Well, in our house, once the chocolate box of life has been passed around, all that's left are the ones that are an acquired taste, the hard nuts and the toffee-nosed. Which accurately describes my feisty, sultry, snooty, lazy, rebellious, stunningly drop-dead gorgeous, snarling darling teenage daughter. Never judge your own mother until your daughter becomes a teenager.

You know you've acquired a modicum of maturity when you can see your mother's point of view – which is even more painful than discovering you can get on your therapist's nerves on the odd occasion.

The sad fact is, even I get on my own nerves every so often. I am at the point in my life where I love my family, but I am so over them. I love my house, but I am so over housework. I love my newly renovated kitchen dearly, but if I lived on my own all I'd eat is soylent green. And I love my garden to bits, but I am so over getting down and dirty with my diosmas.

I also love *Desperate Housewives*, but I am not, by any stretch, over that adorable, sexy, school-age gardener who regularly mows the nature strip at a certain house on Wisteria Lane.

Now there's someone I could hump in the hydrangeas or rollick in the roses with. I'm not about to feel guilty about my menopausal fantasies because my ageing husband is meanwhile waiting by the phone for the call from Jennifer or Nicole to let him know that they are currently footloose and fancy-free.

In the meantime we still have our teenage daughter banging on about how everything in her life is my fault. Just one of the many advantages and privileges of being a mother.

I believe it's tradition for a mother to read her teenage daughter's diary, but, for the same reason I don't look at the sun during an eclipse, I never delve into the drawers or cupboards in my daughter's room.

Never look on the bright side of life; you'll be permanently blinded by what you don't want to find in your teenage daughter's bedroom. Remember, too, that behind every cloud there's, well, there's more clouds, all converging, merging and brewing into a spectacular thunderstorm.

Besides, I don't have to sneak a peek into her diary because she has this sadistic habit of telling me everything that goes on in her life. It makes Wisteria Lane look like Ramsay Street.

Superman never dies

I have a pre-teenage son who thinks he's immortal. He's constantly living on the edge of my comfort zone.

At the age of two he was wearing his pants on the outside of his jeans, jumping off our pergola thinking he could soar into the heavens.

It never happened, but he never stopped believing in himself.

In the meantime, we had to gently remind him that even Superman had to clean his teeth and flush the toilet behind him.

When he was older we bought him a BMX bike and he joined the local BMX club. Rather than racing around the streets and bush tracks charged with adrenaline, we thought joining the club would be a safer alternative.

The first three times I took him there, an ambulance was called for other boys, who also thought they were immortal, but who received a rude shock when their fragile bodies hit the reality of gravel and bitumen.

So we bought our son the best helmet we could find, as well as the best medical insurance we could afford. To protect his brains and his body until he discovered it was his imagination that was limitless, not his flesh and blood self.

When our son decided BMX was too tame he started dreaming about motorbikes. It was never going to happen, but we let him believe it would.

After he exhausted the impossibilities of owning a Harley Davidson in primary school, he got into music. The trombone was his new BMX. He played it in the school concert, and I was so proud.

I had an overwhelming sense of joy and happiness for all the different stages boys go through in order to be like their fathers.

I have a middle-aged husband who knows he can fly – but only with the aid of an airplane and a pilot's licence.

I always wanted to be Superman. I always dreamt I could fly and save the world.

Superman is not a gender – it's a state of mind.

It's up to us as parents to quietly point out to our sons that it is possible to fly through the universe of our mind without actually leaving Planet Earth.

Sometimes we have to sacrifice our own dreams for the sake of our children.

How many of us ever thought Superman would shuffle off this mortal coil?

But he hasn't died.

He's given us all the gift of life.

Superman will always live on in the hearts of our children.

Forever.

Fraught with danger

The most important thing a father can do for his children is to love their mother. And after receiving a twenty year marriage sentence – that's no mean feat.

We're not talking hot and horny, passionate *Titanic* style love. It's more a mutual survival skill necessary to raising three happy and healthy children in the iceberg-filled stormy seas of suburban life.

I sometimes think our family hasn't just clipped the side of an iceberg, it's smashed straight through it and is now hurtling full steam ahead straight towards the entire Antarctic coastline in the shape of our first teenage party.

Our daughter has invited fifty of her closest friends to invade our house on Saturday night. Trouble is – fifty of her closest friends will be text messaging fifty of their closest friends to join in the fun and festivities.

So we were advised by fifty of our closest friends to install a team of security guards at our front door – to keep the riff raff at a safe distance.

Colour me naive or what!

I had no idea that a few sausage rolls and party pies could be fraught with such danger. Back in the seventeenth century, when I celebrated my fourteenth birthday, it was with a Bay City Rollers party.

Decked out in our best tartan clobber, we shang-a-langed the night away – hotly debating whether Woody had a bigger guitar than Eric.

I was warned by her Royal Teenage Highness that I was allowed to serve and slave – but I had to keep a low profile in case I said something to embarrass her, such as, 'Would anyone like more fairy bread before we play pass the parcel?'

When I asked her if karaoke singing an ABBA medley with her father would constitute an embarrassment, she froze me with an icy glare that dropped the room temperature by several degrees and the words 'Gay Retard Sad Super-Freak Loser' hung in the air.

I believe that's teen-speak for, 'Thanks Mum, I love you too.'

However, she not only managed to thaw out later on, but she also positively radiated with warmth when I gave her a teddy bear present. On its tummy, emblazoned in gold was the message: 'I'm not messy. I'm creative.' It wasn't so much a teddy bear as a very subtle hint to tell her to tidy up her bedroom.

These days it's easier to raise the *Titanic* than it is to raise a teenager, which takes a lot of time, effort, commitment and care.

By the way. My very subtle hint went straight over her head. As I knew it would.

All hell breaking loose

Hello. You have reached the Bad Mothers' Crisis Lukewarm Line. Your call is important to you. Your call may be monitored for staff entertainment and piss-taking purposes.

Please choose an option from our Options Menu or hold the line until one of our overpaid, single and childless staff members can be bothered to take your call.

Press 1 if you are still suffering from postnatal depression even though your most recent child is now in high school.

Press 2 for midnight panic attacks because you failed to remember that
- your child needs a Harry Potter costume for Dress Up Day at school tomorrow and you have no idea who Harry Potter is

- your child is having an end-of-term party and you promised to whip up a Bombe Alaska
- your child is graduating from high school
- all of the above
- none of the above – panic attacks happen.

Press 3 if you failed to pick up your child from school last Friday because the Bad Mothers' Lunch turned into the Bad Mothers' Night Out.

Press 4 if you are a neglected husband whose wife is not willing to attend to your physical needs at three o'clock in the morning. It won't cure your sexual frustration, but it'll be something to do with your hands.

Press 5 if you not only want to have your cake and eat it, but you also want to be the chief executive officer of the entire cake shop.

Press 6 if you came home from work, lied to the kids that karate had been cancelled, and then, flopped into a chair with a box of Cadbury's, a bottle of chardonnay and a book about full-time working mothers who get it just as wrong as you do.

Press 7 if you spent six months wages on an X-Box, Game Cube or PlayStation 2 – or all 3 – to alleviate your guilt at ever wanting a life.

Press 8 if you have forgotten what your problem was. Then go back to the hospital where you gave birth and ask if you can have some brain replacement therapy.

We are sorry but you have pressed the wrong button and have now been placed at the back of the queue. Please remember that your call is still important to you.

We will be with you as soon as it is convenient to us.

Thank you for calling the Bad Mothers' Crisis Lukewarm Line.

Sibling rivalry

Mothers are the most powerful creatures on earth, with the ability to brainwash and control minds. And you thought we just cooked, cleaned and shouted every day.

Last week two of my children cared and shared the living daylights out of each other over some burning sibling rivalry issues.

They cared and shared some personal tips on brotherly love with their fists, thumping their personal care factor into each others brains.

I threw a forty-two year old's tantrum.

'Learn some impulse control!' I shouted in their ears. 'Violence and screaming don't solve anything.'

If you thought chess was about moving wooden pieces on a black and white board, you're sadly mistaken. It's about siblings asserting their independence and engaging in a power struggle to annihilate each other off the face of the earth.

It's not how you play the game that counts, it's whether you win or lose. It's your job to teach them that if you are able to lose gracefully, you will always be a winner.

Your boys won't remember if the house was neat and clean at all times but they will remember if you played Snakes and Ladders with them.

Monopolise their time over a board game, then thrash the socks off of them. It's a mother's duty to be cruel to be kind.

Where's the fun in buying your boys a $200 chemistry kit and not letting them blow up their bedrooms? If you can't care and share the explosion, you may as well buy the latest PlayStation and let them blow up the virtual world alone. It's not the latest computer you're buying, it's your own personal space and time. Instant gratification takes too long.

To err is human. To torture your children for an eternity is divine. Rather than torturing your child's inner Toys "R" Us, wave your magic wand and nurture their soul instead and save yourself some money in the process.

Get the best revenge by wanting to spend your precious time with them. It will confuse and baffle the bad behaviour out of them.

Use your powers for good, not evil. Look your children straight in the eye and, with a very low, soothing voice, hypnotise your care factor into them. Please note, this does not work down at the local supermarket.

My children are very important. I have no favourites, I love all of them equally. It's their temper tantrums I can't stand.

Honing your anti-parenting skills

I wish someone could've banged into my thick head just what working motherhood was really like.

I spent ten years as a stay-at-home mother and loved it, but the time came when all three children were in school and I had run out of cupboards to sort out and toilets to clean. So I went back to work part time.

It's a fight getting us all out the door at the same time in the mornings, with an afternoon replay when they come home from school. The main fight is about getting through the front door first. Believe me: no matter how good your calculator, three kids and three schoolbags do not go through one door at the same time. There is always a loser who feels the overwhelming need to thump the other two, who feel the overwhelming need to thump him back.

They thump each other through the house, leaving bags, socks, shoes, hats, and other miscellaneous school-related paraphernalia in their wake as they beat a path to the fridge. After devouring its contents, they settle down to watch *Cartoon Network*.

I sit down with them and ask about their day. After a hard day's graft and corruption I'm under the misguided apprehension that my children actually want to talk to me after school.

'Move, Mum. I can't see the television.'

Of course your children understand and are grateful that you work long hours so they can spend quality time on the PlayStation with *Mario Kart* and *Warped Bandicoot Three*, as well as Foxtel.

Communication is monosyllabic, and that's when their friends aren't there. If they have friends over, my children look straight through me, pretending that I don't really exist.

So we decided that, because weekdays are so stressful, it is better for the entire family to spend the weekend curled up on the settee watching Japanese cartoons rather than race around Perth trying to edutain the children at an assortment of venues.

We all love our children dearly and would lay down our lives for them, but if they annoy us just once more, we will break their train sets.

Socking it to 'em

Do you know what your children get up to behind your back? Right under your nose?

I feel even the most diligent mother, working or not, doesn't have a clue what her children get up to.

It's impossible to follow your school-age children everywhere, and children, like adults, occasionally need secrets from each other.

It's my experience that most of these secrets eventually hit the light of day.

Like the time my two older children made a $5 bet with my youngest son. To win this money he had to wear one pair of socks for a month and they bet him he wouldn't dare to. This wager took place during the height of summer when even one-day-old socks tend to smell like gorgonzola. Call it a science experiment if you like.

All my kids thought that not only was it hilarious that he managed to complete the challenge and collect his $5, but also that I had no idea what was going on under my nose, behind my back.

I came home from work one day to discover that my eight-year-old son had the most horrendous case of tinea, or athlete's foot, and blood blisters on the back of every toe; he must have felt like chopping them all off.

Then I discovered that the rest of the family had varying degrees of tinea.

Suddenly, that pain between my toes finally registered and I felt like the worst mother in the world.

Initially, when the pain first started, I put it down to the fact the showers hadn't been cleaned for a month. I'd recently noticed a rabid fungal growth in the shower and thought I must get around to cleaning it. I forgot that no one else in the house was capable of cleaning the shower – unless, of course, I ranted and raved and threatened to cancel cable television for good.

The only time jobs around the house get done is when I burst a lung.

So, at the end of the month, he had a raging case of blistering tinea on all ten toes. As well as a mother who had a raging case of blistering guilt. But underneath I had to admire his pain tolerance and his staying power.

Said socks were beyond washing. They were so stiff they stood up by themselves and, sensing my severe disapproval, silently tip-toed to the bin and jumped in, just like a pair of lemmings.

But it does beg a question or two. Would this have happened if I were a stay-at-home mum rather than a bad working mother? Would I have noticed the lack of socks as I dumped ten loads in the washing machine on the weekend or would I have carefully allocated five pairs of socks to each child?

I guess we'll never know the answer to that one.

Romancing the phone

My teenage daughter is having a passionate love affair – with her mobile phone.

Actually, it's my old phone. I got a new phone and she got my old one. Yes, the family pecking order sucks.

For about a week she was so excited. For about a week. Then I got complaints that the kids at school were asking for her brick number. A mobile that weighs more than a credit card is not a phone — it's a brick. It is not cool to be asked for your brick number.

So, being parents who do give in to relentless teenage pressure, we got her the almost latest phone. Which will probably keep her happy for a term. Two, if we're lucky, but we've resigned ourselves to getting an update for her birthday. Her brother will inherit the family brick.

Last time I looked, phones were for talking to other people, for imparting valuable information during semi or actual emergencies. I had no idea of the constant source of entertainment a mobile phone could give. Anything that occupies a bored thirteen year old for the annual two week camping holiday has to be worth the money spent.

I recall with nostalgia fire-engine red public phone booths with matching mini-me letter boxes alongside them. Non-vandalised phones were the norm back then. If you didn't have 10 cents to call your parents to come and pick you up, you had two choices: you could ring your parents, reverse the charges and hope your parents accepted the call, or you rang an operator and said you'd lost your money. If you were lucky, the operator would connect you, but if the operators thought you were trying to rort the system, they'd simply hang up. Then you had to resort to shouting down the earpiece in the hope that your parents could hear your faint pleas for transport home.

Mobile phones have taken the fun out of twenty-first century life. Conning a gullible adult into giving you a freebie gave you at least fifty cool points.

Otherwise there was the humiliation of failure, and legging it home was your only option.

Mobile phones disguised as shoes were invented by the *Get Smart* people and owning one was about as remote as Dial-a-Pizza to the average teenager living in the 1970s.

Cordless phones were, in the 1970s, also at least twenty years into the future. You had to conduct your phone conversations, preferably in Teenage Code, within 1 metre of your parents' overextended ears. Your parents attempted to give the impression that they were engrossed in *Gilligan's Island* on the black and white television. I was well into my thirties before I could go to the loo and phone a friend at the same time.

In all innocence – and naiveté – we thought a $10 prepaid card would keep the Optus wolf from our door.

Two months later, we received a $600 bill. Normally $200, we thought it was an Optus mistake, until we scrutinised further.

Our daughter may not have made actual calls, but downloading logos and ring tones was just as costly. It would appear we were lucky. She was apparently quite restrained when compared with a friend whose daughter racked up a $4000 bill.

Mental note: Check out what Telstra and Optus shares are worth. At this rate we'll be able to buy out the company she loves so much.

Upwardly mobile family

We are an upwardly mobile family. An upwardly mobile phone family that is, although sometimes our mobility is in a decidedly downhill fashion.

Each of our three children have mobile phones and spend the best part of their pocket money text messaging each other at the dinner table. That's their choice.

Giving my children freedom to choose is more important to me than what they spend their money on. You could easily call me a slack, indulgent mother – but that's OK; I've been accused of far worse.

In return, my kids give me freedom of choice to mess around with them where I get to feel more like their older sister instead of their mother.

But along with freedom of choice – or slack, indulgent motherhood – comes responsibility, so I repeatedly advised them not to take their phones to school, but I was constantly assured that every child at school has one.

And to be honest, I rather enjoy getting phonecalls at recess and lunchtime from my boys, just checking up to see that their mum is behaving herself. I assured them that I wasn't, of course.

Sometimes kids just need the soothing, comforting sound of their mother's voice so they can get on with their sums – before annoying the hell out of the teacher.

Then, the inevitable happened. My youngest son came home complaining his almost financially depleted simcard was allegedly stolen out of his phone.

Thinking it was a scam to con more money, I eyeballed him at length, waiting for a full confession. It wasn't forthcoming.

So I fobbed him off for a week, making up all sorts of complicated technical reasons why Telstra wouldn't accept a new simcard until the old one was found. Meanwhile he stuck to his guns.

A week later, the police knocked on our door politely enquiring whether anyone had been murdered at our address.

Aside from massacring a chicken casserole I was preparing for dinner that night, no other bloodshed had occurred. It would appear someone had stolen my son's simcard after all and used it to make prank phone calls.

To my son's credit, he didn't say, 'Ner, ner! Told you so', as I would have done in similar circumstances, and I did have the good grace to feel very ashamed for doubting him.

I learnt a valuable lesson in life that night. No – not how to cook the perfect chicken casserole, but to always give my children the benefit of the doubt.

Children seem rarely ever to lie.

Most important – make sure you don't have chicken casserole stains down your jumper when you open the front door. You never know when you might find two burly policemen on your doorstep.

3

Q: are Teenagers and Boundaries mutually exclusive?

A: When Good Mothers Turn Bad

Bad Mother love

How many happy teenagers does it take to change a light globe?

First of all, like money trees and adequate mental health funding, there's no such thing as a happy teenager. Second, they are too lazy to be bothered. And third, most teenagers want to keep their parents in the dark for as long as possible anyway.

Bringing up a teenager is like trying to rollerblade uphill. The harder you try, the more effort you put into it, the further backwards you slide until, finally, you crash into something you didn't see coming.

Apparently, teenagers don't argue with their parents so much as they are learning the delicate art of negotiation and they don't defy boundaries so much as they are learning to assert their independence.

So while I was negotiating my side of their independence at the top of my voice, I discovered that the secret to dealing with outrageous teenage behaviour is to look after yourself.

That was the advice I was given, from teachers and doctors to our local garage attendant. Make sure you get enough sleep, eat healthy food, exercise, and distance and detach yourself from teenage issues while still caring enough to give them a hard time.

Keeping the bar fridge full is also a therapeutic option. Of course, alcohol is not a permanent solution to life's problems. Just a temporary one until you can get a restraining order out on your teenage children.

It's been said to me that teenagers are time-consuming in the strangest of ways and the best way to cope is to put your oxygen mask on first.

Aren't we instructed when we board that if the plane loses altitude and the oxygen masks fall, to get our own mask in place before attempting to put one on our children's face. You can't help anyone else if you're floundering around unable to breathe. All of which is null and void if the plane is about to crash-land in a fireball explosion.

When parenting teenagers becomes all about damage control rather than setting boundaries, some very deep breathing becomes a necessary part of life.

Setting boundaries means banning your teenagers from watching *Big Brother*. Damage control is discussing at the dinner table why two inmates thought it was a good idea to get down and dirty in a bath on national television.

Damage control also means listening to endless fart and body function jokes with a frozen smile on your face. If men are from Mars and women are from Venus, then teenagers are definitely from Uranus.

Watching programs such as *When Hidden Cameras Attack*, and *Ibiza Uncovered* and anything starring Paris Hilton while lying inert on a couch will score you many cool points.

But it's all rather tragic when Jerry Springer becomes the household authority figure and has the last word on everything.

Hospital sweet home

Recently, I decided I needed a break. So I booked into hospital to have an organ removed. God, in his infinite wisdom, gave us mothers a couple of get-out-of-jail-free cards. I have a couple of spare, free-floating organs just ready for that well-deserved emergency holiday.

And who wouldn't enjoy hospital? All that attention by nurturing staff. No children fighting or swearing. No mislaid homework to find. No scouring local mulberry bushes for leaf-eating silkworm pets. No trying to cook creative dinners with just a can of beans and a loaf of bread. In other words, no responsibilities and, when the phone rings, I can actually be sure it's for me.

I get to be lazy and irresponsible, lolling around in my pyjamas in bed all day while someone else cooks my breakfast, lunch and dinner for a change. I also get to see the *Bold and the Beautiful* all the way through. On the down side, I do have to speak to my children on the telephone every night and tolerate the occasional rowdy visit.

But all in all, it's a fine life and someone has to live it.

The best part is I get to have my drugs mainlined instead of just fantasising about them because, let's face it, reality is an illusion caused by a severe shortage of mind-altering drugs. In hospital, all I have to do is press the right button on the right machine for instant happiness.

The drugs were quite wonderful. They even made television infomercials sound intelligent and entertaining and I got all amazed and agitated about the one that demonstrated a product that plastic-wrapped and vacuum-sealed leftover food. I was so excited I rang up to order one. Then the drugs wore off.

But the funny thing is that after a week of being showered with unadulterated and undivided attention, I am more than ready to sign myself out of hospital and back into the loving arms of my dear family.

Until the next time, that is, because I still have a couple of cards up my sleeve in the shape of a dodgy appendix and an even dodgier gall bladder. It's just a matter of time.

Call of the Holy Rollers

It's a teenage dream to be forty-one and to find you're having more fun with your favourite pop group than your teenage daughter is with hers.

In November 2003, Les McKeown's legendary Bay City Rollers rocked into Western Australia and blasted the cobwebs off our dusty state with four capacity-filled concerts, causing our teenage hearts to hammer wildly in our saggy, daggy, middle-aged bodies.

Rollermania hit Perth twice in the 1970s. Aside from being tossed out of the Entertainment Centre by my short and curlies for knee-capping a bouncer, my most enduring memory is of the enterprising fan who jumped on stage, tripped over some wiring, played possum and got dragged to the side by the stressed out St John Ambulance crew, then sprang miraculously back to life and rugby tackled a very startled guitarist, Eric Faulkner, who unwittingly body surfed himself into a raging sea of tartan. The most amazing part was that Faulkner didn't miss a single guitar note, even though the instrument was now firmly fixed around his neck.

Back then you were either a Bay City Rollers fan or a Sherbet fan. You couldn't be both. There were unwritten rules and regulations, and that was one of them.

Every Saturday morning, bemused Hay Street Mall shoppers would be greeted by a sea of tartan on one side and shiny satin suits on the other. The warring factions hissing fighting words and abuse at each other across a huge no man's land down the middle.

I was a closet Daryl Braithwaite fan but kept my tawdry secret to myself. There never has been a safe time to come out. Even now, if middle-aged mothers identify themselves as The Other Side, it's guaranteed you're always going to be wary of each other.

Before the days of remote-controlled videos, a cassette player held up to the television was standard fare for recording television music shows. If our parents or siblings had a blazing row going in the background, it was replayed in magnificent glory every time you tried to listen to your favourite song.

Those were the days when the internet was barely a figment of anyone's imagination. We were still wondering what the colour of Skipper and Gilligan's shirts were and Elton John was still well and truly heterosexual. Computers were the size of a block of flats and cable television was all about watching Barry play football on Saturday afternoons.

My thirteen-year-old daughter is waiting for the 3D Hologram PlayStation 36, which not only beams you instant piping hot pizza and Coke, but also delivers a different life-sized pop concert into her bedroom every night of the week. It's only a matter of time.

Front row concert tickets were not for those with the quickest push button finger and highest credit card limit. One didn't have to refinance the house and send the kids out begging on the streets in order to pay for them. I paid $6.25 for my 455th row ticket back in 1976.

Front row concert tickets were for the brave and fearless and those who possessed the most endurance and stamina to suffer the freezing cold elements, back-breaking concrete pavements and drunken, abusive youths. And that was before reality television.

It was common to see a snaking line of sleeping bags cocooning cold, hungry, sleep-deprived preteens hugging the curved windows of the Entertainment Centre. These were the days before the Duty of Care Act.

I didn't dare lie to my parents about staying at a fictitious friend's house for a week so I could camp outside the Entertainment Centre, so for me the Bay City Rollers was little more than a set of five microscopic tart ants prancing about on stage. There were no huge background video screens.

I spent most of the time jumping up and down trying to flatten shaggy-dog haircuts and dodge football-oval-sized banners proclaiming everlasting love for their favourite Roller, just so I could get the occasional tantalising glimpse of my idols.

I remember the support act creeping timidly onto stage, facing 3500 fuming and seething hormonal teenage girls and announcing 'We're Haystack and we're here to play for half an hour whether you like it or not.'

When we entered the Internet Age in 1998, the first words I and thousands of Western Australian women typed into the search engine were 'Bay City Rollers'. I was stunned to find that, not only were they all still alive – some only just, mind you

– but some were also still performing and playing all their old hits.

The Rollers had split into two warring factions. Now, there was Les McKeown's Legendary 70's Bay City Rollers and Eric Faulkner's The Rollers. Expensive court action was necessary to stop both parties resorting to fisticuffs over the entitlement of the original name. There appeared to be as much love between the ex Bay City Rollers as there was between the Hay Street Maulers.

I attended a Fan Reunion in Edinburgh in 2000 where Les's Legendary band performed a private concert. I finally got front row tickets. Most people don't understand how charismatic and utterly charming Les McKeown is. They dismiss him as a teenybopper has-been who never was. He could have been a cult leader or a politician. Well, same thing really.

At the concert, I witnessed something that I thought existed only in my sad memories of the 1970s. Crowds of screaming girls packed tighter than two coats of paint were pressing themselves up against the 4 centimetre stage. Only they weren't girls any more. They were somebody's wives and mothers.

I felt I was in some sort of crazy, surreal time warp. Some 'girls' were dressed in more tartan than Edinburgh Castle's Changing of the Guard. It was all rather bizarre.

Although I had campaigned with other girls for several years to get a promoter to bring them to Australia, we never really believed it would ever happen. Then, late in 2003 it finally did. Through this promotional work, I had amassed a very respectable crowd of Les's Ladies Who Lunch and now the Tartan Army was ready to march. This included Eric Faulkner's rugby tackler who became my mascot for the recent Australian tour.

I was one of several girls who sold merchandise for the band during the tour. These were the same girls who had flown with me to Edinburgh to finally meet their favourite pin-up boy.

During the month they were in Australia touring, I had to endure three weeks and three days of sheer unadulterated agony before they hit Perth. Hearing from the other girls about how fantastic the concerts were, I was terrified I was going to get hit by a bus and die before they arrived.

At every concert, they totally Rocked the Kasbah. They sang a lot of the originals and had jazzed them up superbly over the years. Most of the audience knew some of the words and the lung-crushing crowd was still the same, just thirty years older.

About two thousand people saw Les perform over four consecutive nights. All the fans, without exception, were impressed with Les's energy and on-stage personal interaction with the fans.

I can guarantee that all the people who saw the concert will return to see them again.

There was the added bonus of an autograph session after the concert and Les and the boys spent plenty of time with the fans talking to them and signing memorabilia from the 1970s. On one memorable night I was his personal bodyguard and had to make sure no one, except myself, got too close to him.

On another night, the band was ushered out of the venue prematurely, leaving three fans with personal signature guaranteed merchandise, impersonally unsigned. One girl burst into tears and threw a hysterical tantrum worthy of Liam Gallagher on a Qantas flight.

This was the fabled and mythical girl who, in a valiant effort to wrap herself around Eric Faulkner's neck, inadvertently wrapped his rhythm guitar around it instead.

We took her details and organised a free autographed CD for her to collect when she came along to the last concert of the tour. Les likes to come off stage during the concert and single out some lucky girl for a bit of personal attention.

He thoroughly enjoys this interaction while performing and even gets them to sing into the microphone with him. This time, he came off stage and, with a look of blissful ignorance on his face, approached Eric Faulkner's worst nightmare.

He was completely unaware of preceding events and spent ages flirting with her. The look of rapture on her face was priceless. It was only after the concert that he found out who she was. Due to the acrimonious nature of the history with his former band member he was well and truly impressed with her efforts.

I'm not sure if I was incredibly disappointed or immensely relieved when they flew back to England and we were free to resume our now very average lives.

I had spent four days living on adrenaline and virtually no sleep. In the meantime, my family had subsisted on two-minute noodles until it all got too much and they unanimously decided to pack the tent and move as far away as possible from all the action. Outer Mongolia was still too close for comfort.

My daughter did a survey among her friends and they decided all mothers should simply stay home to cook and clean. However, my two boys can't decide if I am very weird in a cool way, or very cool in a weird way, and they are extremely confused as to who the teenager in the house is. My children beg me and promise to do their homework if I give up singing Bay City Roller songs at the top of my voice.

Both my daughter and her brothers cringe low in the back seat of our car as I wind down the window and wildly sing the

Legendary version of 'S.A.T.U.R.D.A.Y. Night' as we pull up in front of their friend's place.

We must be the only house in the Universe where the long-suffering teenager shouts at her mother to turn the music down.

Of course, there are some people who think I have totally flipped my tam-o-shanter and should be locked up until I learn how to act my age.

Since the tour, fan gatherings have been springing up like the Flower of Scotland in every state and territory of Australia. Friendships have been made and firmly sealed over the bonding experience of watching Mr McKeown strut his stuff on stage.

Schoolfriends have rediscovered each other bopping away to 'Summerlove Sensation' at concerts, the same way they did back in the 1970s.

I feel sorry for anyone who isn't a Bay City Rollers fan.

Like mother, like daughter

My snarling, darling daughter bodysurfed the mosh pit at the recent Rock-It concert. Now she thinks she's too cool for her classroom and too hip to do her homework.

Sadistically, I reminded her of the time I took her to see Humphrey B Bear in concert and that he loomed so much larger than life on her horizon that she wet her pants. OK, so she was only three at the time.

Then I reminisced about the time I jet-propelled myself over several rows of seats in order to get up close and personal with David Cassidy. OK, so I was forty at the time. But at least my pants stayed dry. Just.

My mother accompanied me to Cassidy's 1974 Perth concert, where his white cat suit was so tight I could clearly see the outline of his electric guitar. I wondered if the tight white cat suit might have made a 2002 appearance at the Burswood Theatre, but, like multicoloured buses and that 1970s hairstyle, the shaggy mullet, some things are best left behind.

So when the telepathic moment that occurs at most pop concerts arrived – where all the sad people rush the stage – myself and a hundred other psychic middle-aged women clambered over the flimsy seating arrangement to get to the front, rather like a herd of shopaholics thundering through Myer during the January sales.

I elbowed and barged my way to the stage, gazed up adoringly into his eyes and held my hand up to be touched by his magical, mystical powers.

'*Let go!*' David Cassidy – childhood idol, up very close and very personal – screamed in my face. I let go, mortified beyond belief that I'd somehow surgically attached myself to his hand and refused to let go. My face went red and my armpits itched in embarrassment. It was far, far worse than getting tossed out by my short and curlies at a Bay City Rollers concert.

However, I felt much better when several other women were also screamed at by his Royal Retroness because they, too, wanted a piece of him – and not necessarily his hand either.

I'm just glad my dear old Mum wasn't there; she would have been ashamed of my lack of restraint. If she were ever to say anything about my behaviour, I'll just have to remind her of her day in the sun when she used to scream and throw her knickers at Tom Jones.

Like Mother, like Daughter, like Grandmother. We're just not happy unless we're screaming at somebody.

Whip it good

The other day on Discovery Channel I watched a program devoted to the excruciatingly painful initiation rites and ceremonies of various cultures around the world. Facial tattoos, piercings, poisonous ant bites and thirteen-year-old boys whipping the skin off each other's back. He who cries first, loses. There is no second place.

All rather reminiscent of Richard Harris being hung out to dry by his nipples in an initiation ceremony scene from *A Man Called Horse*. I've got my hands clamped over my chest just thinking about it.

It's not like we women can't feel his pain. Breastfeeding mums average about six months hanging theirs out in all sorts of weather. I know what a detached nipple feels like.

It would appear men detach for fun and women detach because they have to. It occurred to me that the men in our house conducted similar initiation ceremonies all in the name of fun.

A while ago my husband and two boys spent the best part of an hour whipping each other with tea-towels after dinner while my teenage daughter and I cheered them on from the sidelines. Things hotted up when I suggested the participants take off their T-shirts and wet the ends of the tea-towel in order to prove their manhood.

Now I know why Roman gladiator sports were so popular.

As each son and their father vied for top-dog position in our household, our Maltese terrier barked and ran around in circles creating her own ritualistic ceremony.

The two cats watched the proceedings from where they were sprawled on the top of the fridge, a lofty position that clearly delineated their royal status within the household. Their disdainful expressions depicted that they thought that the dog was in desperate need of pet therapy.

Eventually, all three bare-breasted contestants ended up a heaving, sweating, panting bonded heap of testosterone on the kitchen floor with some very serious welts happening.

I think a few scores got settled that hour as well.

I threw my husband a clean tea-towel and said, 'Want to feel like a real man? Put my apron on and do those dishes.'

Then I went off to perform my own pain-filled sacrificial ritual with an exfoliating scrub, some tweezers and a pot of hot wax.

We desperate housewives are no shrinking violets when it comes to pain; rather, we are tall, strong sunflowers, flexible and bending in the wind.

We take many a trip to the hairdresser's or beauty salon, where we go in looking like Godzilla's love child and come out looking like Farrah Fawcett Majors. As one of my friends declared, 'It takes a lot of time, pain and money to look this natural.'

Scary fairy stories

I'm going to give up smoking

There's nothing scarier than a Bad Mother with a debilitating case of nicotine withdrawal. I used to buy cigarettes and cover the health warnings on the packet with stickers that said 'Smoking is Cool'. Now, I'm desperately trying to give up smoking. To help myself, I've switched to Nicobate chewing gum. Trouble is, chewing gum is very hard to light.

It's a medical marvel that someone who's had a hysterectomy can still suffer from pre, post and present menstrual tension, which is what giving up smoking feels like to me.

Scary things happen when Mum gives up smoking and her kids give her the irrits. Just remember, she might not be able to light up her chewing gum, but she sure as hell can smoke out any bad thoughts on insurgent behaviour you might be having.

Back in the psychedelic 1960s, when everyone smoked, I used to worship Bill and Ben the Flowerpot Men who loved and nurtured the Weed who lived between them.

I was so naïve back then that I thought 'Lucy in the Sky with Diamonds' was about a girl with a rather pretty name who wore some very expensive jewellery.

I was heavily into heroines at the time, my favourite being George, the transvestite from Enid Blyton's Famous Five. Enid Blyton was one Bad Mother. She used to neglect her own children so she could write books for other people's darlings.

I never could, with any seriousness, read those stories to my children. Cousin Dick and Aunt Fanny just used to crack them up, just as Butt Ugly Martians does now. Thanks to Enid Blyton they are well and truly forever stuck in their Freudian Genital Stage.

I gave up on Blyton when I couldn't convince my children that there really were fairies at the bottom of our garden. I knew, because I'd actually seen them. Her fairy books were the mainstay of my childhood.

When I read my favourite fairy stories to my children, they just looked sideways at me, pointed with their finger to their left ear and circulated the finger before backing out of the lounge room.

As far as they were concerned I was talking out of my Butt Ugly Martians.

So I took advantage of the situation and told them I was off to have a smoke behind the shed and spend some quality time with Weed among the Flowerpot Men and, hopefully, we'll catch up with the fairies at the bottom of my garden. And, as far as I'm concerned, SpongeBob SquarePants is your uncle.

Guilt-framed pictures of my family

Mothers are hard-wired for guilt.

I used to wake up in the middle of the night in a cold sweat because my four-year-old daughter could not colour inside the lines. I took her to the Parent Help Centre. The counsellor told me I needed to de-stress by the time she was of school age, otherwise we could be in for some very rocky times.

When my two boys arrived on the scene, I could not get my head around the fact that some boys just don't do colouring in.

As for my daughter, I solved that particular problem by colouring in for her.

Around about that time, the men in white coats took me away to a nice place where I could colour in to my heart's content.

I thought I was the only one who felt like this until I guiltily admitted my sin to other mothers and found they had also stressed about their preschoolers' artistic talent – or lack thereof. It was a vast relief to know that I was far from being the only mother who coloured in their children's homework.

Logic has nothing to do with the fact that I get the guilts if my child is not doing well at school. I take the blame for it: either I have done something wrong or I have failed to do something crucial as a mother.

I can feel guilty about anything. Then I feel guilty about feeling guilty. All that guilt is pressing me, with immense gravitational force, into the ground. Logic has nothing to do with it.

While some mothers, like myself, crucify themselves over their guilty feelings, some fathers, such as my husband, seem to take the more philosophical view that guilt is a simply a wasted emotion. It would never occur to my husband to colour in my daughter's homework.

The meaning of cleaning

It would be less painful to poke myself repeatedly in the eye with a sharp stick than to go through what I did last week – which is an interview at an employment agency where I discovered just how incompetent, useless and outdated my office skills were. This is where desperate creativity triumphed over sheer bloody desperation.

I discovered that just because I can access pornographic PowerPoint presentations on the internet, it does not mean I should tick that as a proficient skill on my job application form.

It's been fifteen years since I set foot in a real office. Call centres don't count. As I walked down St Georges Terrace for my job interview I felt about as comfortable as Kath and Kim at a Royal Wedding.

The worst part is that everyone there seems to have a job – everyone except for you. Then, the people at the employment agency ask: Why do you want this job?

Well, to be perfectly honest – I don't want this job. I don't like getting out of bed in the morning. What I do like is lunching with friends, followed by an afternoon snooze to help sleep off the strawberry champagne before the kids get home from school. However, as much as that appeals to me, I'm not really looking for a job in politics. I left the employment agency feeling as though I had farted in the foyer.

My first job post-children was office cleaning. When I informed my kids they said in a collectively awed voice that I must really love cleaning if I wanted to do it as a job as well.

But I'm over cleaning, both in the house and as a potential career. I'm over picking up, cleaning behind, dusting off, putting away and generally mollycoddling my three rapidly growing ingrates. And I tell them so.

After all, the hand that rocks the cradle also rocks the boat. I'm also over scraping pizza toppings off the kitchen ceiling and scouring the toilet, especially after an all-male slumber party for my just-turned-twelve-year-old son.

Is there life beyond the kitchen sink? When your oven is filthy, is it better to buy a new one or sell the house? Will the Universe collapse if I don't wash my kitchen floor every day? Is there a meaning to cleaning, and just what actually is a self-cleaning oven anyway? Is it the same as a self-cleaning house that most husbands with stay-at-home wives come home to every night?

I didn't get the real job – as opposed to my fake job as a wife and mother. What I did get was a good dose of post-traumatic stress disorder for my trouble.

That night as I washed the dishes and made my husband a cup of tea, I thought, 'It's nice to know I have a Certificate of Proficiency in something.'

Bad Mother's revenge day

Mother's Day is little more than a commercial bonanza for dubious retailers to offload useless items at ridiculously inflated prices.

What Women Really Want – is a cup of tea and burnt toast in bed, served on a tray of new-wave, radical, Dalai Lama style approach to family life.

Why is the pursuit and capture of peace and quiet in a household of five a deluded exercise in futility?

Civil war explodes when someone's bubble gum is reported missing in action but the bowl of pistachio nuts on *my* desk with *my* name on them has been designated as communal property.

It's not fluffy fluorescent slippers I desperately crave on Mother's Day, it's personal space – and a ceasefire on the constant dipping and delving into the pistachio nuts of my soul.

When asked to perform simple household tasks in a swift manner, my ten year old, despite the fact that he suffers from obscenely robust health, launches into an impassioned monologue of his life threatening ailments. When facing his own need for speed, he customises and revolutionises his beloved BMX bike into a turbo-charged airborne machine quicker than you can say, 'Are you with HBF?'

Of deeper concern is my other son, whose favourite pastimes include conducting science experiments with magnets and levitation, collecting seeds and growing orchards in his lunchbox and firing off letters of advice to Prime Minister John Howard concerning the state of our nation, but who is intellectually incapable of understanding the basic need for personal hygiene.

And my otherwise intelligent boys fail to appreciate that I get extremely irritable when woken up with the continuous chanting of, 'Are you awake, Mum?'

Another disquieting factor is my daughter's intense passion for foreign languages.

Her opinion regarding a McDonald's-based job is pretty much in neutral, but her enthusiasm for securing employment as a language interpreter at the United McNations is full steam ahead. Why, then, do I have difficulty getting more than a mere mumble of barely discernable English out of her?

My daughter needs to comprehend a few facts of bathroom life. Her thirteen-year-old face does not need the youthful revitalising properties of my very expensive age-defying foundation, which she uses with abandon.

And her electric toothbrush and $3000 braces are a disastrous combination. There won't be a smile on her dial when the braces wires are tightly wrapped around her foundation-covered face.

For 364 four days a year I cook and clean, wash and iron, sweep and vacuum, scream and shout. The only discernable difference about Mother's Day is that I get a free cup of lukewarm tea to soothe my sore throat.

The Dalai Lama's inspirational philosophies and impressive wisdom is universally acknowledged, but I would be breathtakingly awe-inspired if he managed to achieve this significance with three children in tow.

Now *that* would be truly impressive.

Horse-lipped

It amazes me how children know everything. Even when it's crystal clear they're stumbling in the dark, they'll turn around and say, 'I know.'

Last year, we decided to add horse riding to the collective family resume.

Getting on a horse is hard. Staying on is even harder. It occurred to me that if the world were a logical place, men would've ridden side-saddle all those years ago.

The riding instructor gave us a lecture and my children listened intently, in a way they certainly didn't to their parents.

My youngest son had his feet all wrong in the stirrup. Every time I gently but firmly offered my young son advice, he replied (with a sum total of twenty five minutes experience under his belt), 'I know how to ride a horse! Durr!'

As the person who gave birth to him, I didn't want to see him dragged behind the horse if it bolted. I told him where to put his feet and he promptly told me where to put my advice.

The riding instructor turned around and gently but firmly said, 'Listen here, Sonny Boy. Listen to your mother. She knows.'

Much as I dearly love my son, it was very gratifying to see him well and truly slink down in his saddle. I suppressed an overwhelming urge to say, 'Ner, ner, told you so.'

As the second most experienced rider on the trail (my son being the first) I was allowed to canter.

Cantering on a horse is a bit like driving a racing car at 300 kilometres an hour and suddenly realising that it's not that the brakes haven't actually failed, but they simply weren't there in the first place. You know that, eventually, you're going to reach your destination, it's just a matter of when and how.

So I cantered up the hill towards my waiting family. Reaching the summit, I couldn't fail to notice all three of my children were picking their jaws up off the grass. It would appear their mother could actually do something other than cook, clean and shout. She could Ride a Horse. Just like Clancy of the Overflow. I had actually impressed my children.

Let me repeat that in case you missed it – I actually impressed my children.

A shining oven?

An immaculate bathroom?

A well-presented gourmet meal?

These things didn't invoke anything like the awe that thundering up a hill on a mounted steed did.

So I basked in my own guts and glory for the rest of the day until my family shouted at me to shut up.

My husband had the last word. 'You're not a horsewoman, you're just an old nag.'

4

Q: aRe YOU a FISheRWOMaN OR a GOLF aDDICT?

A: Putting the 'Fun' Back Into Dysfunctional

Hooked, line and golfer

As a child I used to go fishing – but the quiet, reflective nature needed to sit still for hours on end didn't belong to me. I was far too impatient. If a fish didn't hook itself onto my line every thirty seconds I was wasting my time.

But just recently I found myself getting older – as one tends to do every so often. I found myself getting older and wiser down by a river in Denmark. It was here that I came to the realisation that the world could be divided into two camps: Fishermen and Golfers. When I was younger, life was a Very Serious Game of Golf.

Now that I'm technically considered to be just past middle age I can quite happily sit by the banks of a river all afternoon and just watch the sun sparkle and bounce off the water.

My husband and two boys are born fishermen. They love the lure and the chase of catching something, anything – even a blowie will do. It's the hunter-gatherer instinct. The three of them spend an excessive amount of time sorting out the contents of their fishing box arguing and debating over which hook to catch which sort of fish is best.

Golf is also a primitive instinctual pastime. Getting that little white ball into a tiny hole in as few strokes as possible is the aim, of course, a hole in one being the ultimate achievement.

In my opinion, there's no such thing as a relaxing game of golf until you hit the nineteenth hole.

Same as there's no such thing as an impatient fisherman. I've watched my two boys just sit on the banks of the river, their eyes glazed over as they contemplate their inner Power Ranger.

Fishing seems to be an excuse to sit and do very little while pretending to be on full alert.

Golf seems to be an excuse to run around in ever-decreasing circles while trying to appear totally relaxed and completely in control.

I've spent enough of my life running around in circles chasing answers to never-ending questions. Now, I'm far more content sitting with my beloved family, quietly watching them contemplate just exactly what life means to them.

The only problem that arises is that each child has to catch a fish before we pack up to go home – otherwise we'll never hear the end of it.

What men want

What men really want for Father's Day is a self-mowing lawn. A 3 metre fishing rod that catches 5 metre sharks off the beach at Hillarys Marina. A maintenance-free house and garden.

A maintenance-free wife with a volume control. A plasma television with a hundred and fifty Foxtel channels, one hundred and forty-nine of which are solely devoted to sport, sport and more sport.

A self-replenishing beer fridge. The ability to grow a luxuriant beard overnight. A bank account with a six figure balance and a four-wheel-drive that can take a severe bush bashing without getting a single scratch.

What men don't want is another pair of Sylvester or Tweety Pie boxer shorts to match the other six never-worn pairs. Sentences from the wife that start off with 'When are you going to fix the —— (insert appropriate fixable item)'. They don't want an audit from the Australian Taxation Office or the latest blockbuster from Marion Keyes or a twelve month subscription to any do-it-yourself magazine or personalised number plates that read 'Under the Thumb' or 'Wifey's Toy Boy'.

The perfect Father's Day involves a trip to the cinema to watch any movie starring Clint Eastwood or Arnold Schwarzenegger, preferably both, in order to further stave off an impending midlife crisis. A day nag-free from the other half, along with the directional powers to get from Eneabba to Timbuktu in their scratch-resistant Land Cruiser without ever needing to consult the road map.

The perfect Father's Day does not involve excitedly unwrapping a book with the title *So You're About to Become a Father for the Fourth Time*, shortly followed by the discovery of a positive pregnancy test in the ensuite rubbish bin.

It does not involve an email from overseas relatives surprising you with the announcement they are arriving in Australia tomorrow and asking if they could sponge off you for the next six weeks. Nor does it involve a credit card statement demanding a four figure sum.

What dad will actually get is a cup of extra strong instant coffee and a piece of cold toast with 3 centimetres of Vegemite at six in the morning, a pair of lurid pink fluffy socks and a box of soft-centred chocolates from his ulterior-motivated teenage daughter, as well as an invitation to conduct a science experiment involving flammable substances from his two primary school-aged sons.

Aren't you glad Father's Day comes around only once a year?

Oh Christmas tree, oh Christmas tree . . .

I bowed to the inevitable last night, pulled myself off the couch, put down the most excellent book I was reading, took a deep breath and braced myself.

There could be no more procrastinating. It was now or never.

So I poured myself a large glass of Christmas cheer, admitted that it was time to get with the program, called the kids and hubby into the lounge room and announced, 'It's time we put up the Christmas tree.'

Christmas starts to sneak into my awareness around about the second week of December. I've always refused to acknowledge the not-so-subtle presence of Christmas in August.

Sticking my fingers in my ears and singing 'Jingle bells, Batman smells' can stave off the fun and festivities for just so long.

So we dragged out the tree, the tinsel and the ornaments and fought over the best way to put it up. We decided that it didn't really matter that much if it was a bit skewiff as the kittens would either topple the tree or end up replacing the angel as twin fairy pussies. Now there's the start of a new tradition.

The best part of the evening was listening to my darling son play Christmas carols on his trombone, knowing that he really didn't sound like a moose dying, as my other two children said he did.

It's a mother's privilege to see the world through rose-coloured glasses when it comes to her children, even if I could visualise a huge hairy beast writhing frantically in the sleet and snow when my other two children, much less subtle, made loud moose-dying noises. I had to stuff the Christmas stocking in my mouth so my giggles wouldn't hurt the trombone-playing son's feelings.

So, with the Christmas tree up and running, we decided it was time to make paper chains and stick them to the walls, thereby ensuring a brand new paint job early next year.

Doing something creative and constructive together is an excellent time to bond with your kids. The repetitiveness lulls them into a false sense of security and, before you know it, you have become privy to your children's deepest, darkest secrets. Such as my ten-year-old son telling me that he hopes that John Howard, who is his hero, will stay prime minister forever, and that not only is 'Advance Australia Fair' his favourite song, but that he also likes to sing it whenever he is alone in the house. Being told your children's secrets is like receiving an early Christmas present.

As to taking down the tree, well, it's supposed to be bad luck to have your Christmas tree up for more than twelve days post Christmas.

So what does that say for us as a family when one year the tree was still standing the following March?

Anyone who asked was told we were just getting in a little bit early this time.

Christmas presents

Christmas is no longer lurking quietly around the corner; it's now hurtling down upon us faster than Santa's sleigh and soon we'll be tucking into Christmas breakfast.

Eating at a fancy restaurant on 25 December to avoid chewing your way through the dry, stringy turkey your mother insisted on cooking used to be considered pure sacrilege, but now it's acknowledged by many that it makes life a lot easier, so that's what we do.

I've made life a lot easier for my husband as well. He's not to buy me anything that plugs in, but a battery-operated power tool you can't buy at Bunnings is a very viable alternative to fluffy towels and a new ironing board.

Monumental changes have been happening in the toy department since I was a knee-high nipper.

For the funky squad, Bratzworld is the most wicked set of integrated teenage-looking dolls and accessories for ages six and over. Accessories include a matchmaker journal and organiser that enables you to analyse your own personality and keep your love life organised. Furniture includes a couch that looks suspiciously like the one in my therapist's office, possibly where six year olds will end up if they actually have a love life that is so disorganised it needs a journal to put it in order.

When a Brat has a problem with her love life and has journalled and organised it, she can then text message her friends and ask their advice on what to do next with the Bratz instant messenger.

When I was six I had a Tiny Tears doll who wet her pants and cried real tears, something I seem to be doing a lot of myself, lately.

For the boys we have a talking Darth Vader head, which, when placed on your head, utters immortal lines from the original movie such as 'Your powers are weak!', 'There is no escape!' and 'Don't make me destroy you!'.

Sounds like the phone call I had from my mother the other day.

One toy from yesteryear that is still popular is the mesmerising Slinky made of tight, spiralling metal that comes to life when palmed from one hand to the other making a metallic slinketty sound that appears to produce a trance-like state in children.

Yes, I'll have three of those please.

Monopoly is one game we have renewed over the years. My kids love playing it. But I was under the impression it was a non-contact, non-violent board game.

As my kids would say, 'Fully sick, Mum!' Something I plan on being around about dinner time on Christmas Day.

Sleeping like a baby

I read an article recently on learning how to sleep like a baby. Trouble is – who wants to sleep like a baby? Waking up screaming every two hours with a full nappy is not my idea of a good night's sleep.

Sleep deprivation is, of course, the oldest form of torture in the book. So is having three children under five years of age.

For anyone contemplating motherhood, or fatherhood for that matter, spend at least five nights in a row setting your alarm clock to go off every sixty minutes during the wee small hours of the morning. Then, pick up a bag of wet cement each time and rock it backwards and forwards for at least three-quarters of an hour. Then, try to get fifteen minutes of quality, uninterrupted sleep before the alarm goes off again.

I even attempted the controlled crying method, in which you leave your baby crying for extended periods of time, but it was me who spent the night crying uncontrollably in front of the television long after my baby had fallen asleep. After that I decided that controlled crying was overrated.

According to the article I read, the answer to insomnia is to not think and to achieve an infant-like state of mind. In other words, think like a baby – or a husband. Husbands and babies have only two things on their mind – breasts and bottles.

You can ring for an appointment at a Professional Sleep Workshop where the whole point is to zone out and fall asleep during lectures.

But it's not thinking like a baby you should be doing, it's thinking like a cat. You'll never find a cat needing professional help to get some shut-eye.

Our cats sleep all day in the sunny part of our lounge room, wake up, stretch and yawn, shed some fleas, demand their nutritional rights, do a post-dinner bowel evacuation in one of my favourite pot plants, and then go back to sleep in front of the fire.

Sleep deprivation can lead to all sorts of shameful, infantile behaviour.

I did a Russell Crowe dummy spit once during a bout of insomnia in which I slammed off the doona, romper stompered out of bed and deliberately side-swiped my sleeping husband. All because I desperately needed to abuse someone and, unfortunately, there wasn't a hotel receptionist in sight.

Children's movies

There's one thing that should be banned from cinemas showing children's movies, and that's children. Either that, or issue anyone over forty with a cattle prod as they enter.

Seeing as I'm getting past my use-by date I need a power nap every time I sit down for more than half an hour, so a poke with a cattle prod would be handy for keeping me awake during long boring movies. And let's face it, a good movie is hard to find these days. A good adult one that is.

Back in the 1970s, I saw *Earthquake* (in Sensor-round) in possibly the most uncomfortable cinema in the Southern Hemisphere, the Grand Theatre, Murray Street, Perth. Sensor-round was touted as the original virtual reality.

I can remember feeling never so ripped off in all my life when I left the Grand Theatre with internal organs and limbs still intact, but a tedious headache and a loud ringing noise in my ears instead.

It was that other disaster movie, *The Towering Inferno*, that really floated my *Poseidon Adventure*.

I had never heard a swear word in a movie before and I was titillated to bits when I heard Steve McQueen utter that immortal four letter word: 'Sugar. Honey. Ice. Tea.'

It goes without saying that teenage fans of the *Die Hard* trilogy will have no idea what I mean by that. If you took out all the swearing, Bruce Willis's part in those movies would be no more than seven minutes long.

I accidentally wandered into a mothers and babies only movie session once and watched *The Sixth Sense* with a bunch of screaming babies. I should have had the sixth sense to leave before the movie started, but seeing as my other five senses are not the sharpest at the best of times, I stayed.

Kids' movies are the best. Although you don't really need to take a child with you for a bit of credibility, I took my double-digit birthday boy along to see *Madagascar*.

It was there I witnessed some very bad behaviour. Feet up on the seat in front, popcorn throwing competitions and, horror of horrors, a mobile phone being answered. It was only when my ten year old pointed out that I was embarrassing him that I stopped.

Two hours is a very long time to expect someone to stay awake, but the movie was so good, the cattle prod was deemed unnecessary.

Although I could have used it on the two families in front of me. I brought one token kid along for the ride, but they managed to bring what appeared to be an entire kindergarten class.

Aside from Supernanny lurking in the aisles hunting for insurgent children, the next best thing would be to screen adults only sessions every time a children's movie comes along.

Mechanically blinded

Our car packed up the other day and, seeing as I am not an expert on cars, or any other subject for that matter – just a know-it-all – we called in the professionals.

Now I know my way around the interior of a car, the petrol gauge, the fluffy dice, the rearview mirror for make-up application and the speedometer, although I'm not so sure about that last one because I would have sworn I was doing 75 in an 80 zone last week, but this blinding flash from the side of the road confirmed otherwise. And I can lift up the bonnet and say 'Yes, that's definitely the engine!'

I also know that when that annoying little red battery light comes on there is something wrong with the battery. But it couldn't be the battery, could it? We had a new one put in just recently. When my car finally ground to a halt, we discovered it wasn't the battery; it was some other thingamajig that fires up the engine.

Of course, what I should have done is gone out and bought a new car to go with the new battery. Our car is entering its teenage years and, like most teenagers, costs a lot of money and gives us nothing but trouble.

I'm just as baffled by the mechanics of a car as I am by the antics of my teenagers. Even though we've brought up the car since it was a baby, I just don't speak its language or make that bonding connection. Although I'm very attached to my car and my teenagers, they both drive me around the bend on a regular basis.

Like a teenager, my car is hard to get started in the morning, guzzles 40 litres of juice every seven days, needs to look good in a crowd and prefers the radio on full blast.

Finally, Mum's Taxi, a typical suburban stationwagon, was off the road for a couple of days yet the kids still didn't get why I couldn't drive them to school. 'Just use the jumper leads,' they shouted. They also didn't get that you need another car to jump start the original one.

My sister drives a brand new, canary-yellow, two-door sportscar, which purrs single, available and no time-consuming grotty, irritating emotional baggage in the shape of kids.

My car screams married with three grotty, irritating children, tired, run-down, fed up and just crying out for a midlife crisis.

My husband drives his midlife crisis to work every day, a brand new Nissan Patrol, while I continue to soldier on with my mechanical teenager.

Personally, I think my car is in its dotage. In car years, it's very close to retirement. But, unfortunately, like the Australian government, I need to flog this particular dead horse for a few years yet.

Supernanny vs Bad Mother

I used to be a professional babysitter. In those days I knew everything there was to know about bringing up children, my major qualification being that I didn't have any.

In fact, I used to think I was a bit of a Supernanny. You know, like Jo Frost. She doesn't have any children. She just sits on her big, fat couch dispensing words of wisdom to the sleep-deprived, as if all these parents don't have a clue about bringing up their own children. All that and I didn't even have my own television show.

In those days, I was faster than a projectile vomit, more powerful than painstop, able to leap over the Lego box in a single bound.

Look! Up in the sky! Is it absurd? Is it a pain? No, it's Supernanny.

Reality television bears little resemblance to, well, reality and being a parent is a bit like fossicking in the dark for a light switch — you eventually stumble across it only to find out it doesn't work.

Perhaps we should live our lives by candlelight, the same way the *Little House on the Prairie* family used to. It took me many years to realise that Mary and Laura Ingalls were actresses reading from a script and not real people and the only thing I ever had in common with Ma and Pa Ingalls was that we both once had three children under five.

That was the era when I spent most of my time in the laundry washing nappies and my husband's shirts — although sometimes not in the same wash — and it suddenly occurred to me that disposable nappies were not evil after all.

From then on it was all about making life easier for everyone. I started to rock my babies to sleep with a honey-covered dummy. Unfortunately, I had to give them away when my teeth started to rot.

It was much easier to send myself to the naughty corner for some good old-fashioned reflection on why I wanted three children in the first place.

When I was single I used to think I was going to die a virgin. When I got married I thought I was going to die without having any children.

Now I just want to be left in peace to reminisce and idealise the good old days, some time in the last century, before my children learnt to walk and talk, when Supernanny and other mythical creatures, along with reality television, simply didn't exist.

Ma wars

A long time ago, in a galaxy far, far away, my best friend and I went to see a virtually unheard of movie called *Star Wars*. Before the year was out we'd seen it thirty times.

Twenty-eight years later, I escaped from my lunatic asylum, disguised myself as a forty-three-year-old mother, joined the twentysomething throng of grunge people and discovered the truth behind Darth Vader.

It was all his mother's fault.

Darth Vader has some very serious unresolved mother issues (as does George Lucas). But instead of being forced to attend anger management classes, he nearly ended up ruling the Universe.

And he would have, were it not for his only son, Luke Skywalker, who intervened and, after chopping off Darth's arm, killed him out of kindness and compassion before being reunited with his twin sister, Princess Leia, the only other remaining Jedi knight.

And you thought *Star Wars* was all about the special effects.

Once, when I had – let's call it – an out-of-body experience, I truly believed I was a Jedi knight and that someone much higher up on the food chain than me was the Jedi Master. But it might be an idea to keep that one to myself.

Back in the seventeenth century, when *American Tiger Beat* and *16* magazine were the hottest items at the newsagent, I was still looking for Bay City Rollers articles when I came across this new movie starring the two grooviest hunks imaginable.

Out went all my Bay City Rollers' paraphernalia. Into the back of Dad's trailer and off to the tip. Sold all my records and bought a ticket to the advance screening.

Of course, we could not be in love with the same character. It contravened the girl rules that only girls understand. Like my teenage daughter, whose group of friends are not allowed to like (let alone buy the CD of) the same band. It's a girl thing – trust me.

So she liked Han Solo and I fell in love with Luke Skywalker. I think I must have been the only person in Perth to read the books before the movie, so I knew all the hot goss before she did, but I had to keep my mouth shut, otherwise, like Luke and Darth, I, too, would have had my arm amputated.

So I kept quiet, unlike a very dear friend who went to see *The Crying Game* before me and said, 'Now who would have thought she would turn out to be a he.' I kept my trap well and truly shut.

Funnily enough, we are still good friends. Just like the Laurel and Hardy act, just like R2D2, the adroit, dry, droll droid, and C3PO.

By the way, just for the record – C3PO is not gay, he's British. May the force be with you.

5
Q: Teachers. heroes or villains?

A: Schooldaze, Holidaze, Confused and Dazed

Reading, writing and respect

Teaching is a spiritual calling. Recently, I ran into an old school friend who had become a teacher.

'What do you teach?' I asked.

'Horrible, badly behaved kids.'

I had no idea she taught at my children's school.

My own spiritual calling is well known at our local school – and at our local bottle shop.

My old friend's sentences don't consist of writing with chalk on the blackboard. Rather, they consist of maximum-security quantity time, educating our future doctors, lawyers and prime ministers, making sure they don't stick their pencils up their noses.

When the school bell rings, it's only a short drive to her next sentence – minimum-security home confinement, where she has to cook dinner and clean house for her supervising officer, wash and iron his self-esteem, and dust and polish his inflated sense of importance – all before retiring to her cell for the night.

Never assume anything: just because your fledgling brood has finally grown up and flown the nest, don't think you have been granted an unconditional pardon. It doesn't exist and the parole board would laugh its head off if you ever applied.

I still feel an overwhelming sense of trepidation and guilt when I speak to teachers and principals about my children these days, the genesis of which dates back to the mid 1970s, when I spent much of my school life pinned by the steely glare of the headmistress and choking on her cigarette smoke.

Only her desk separated me from her desire to give me six of the best for getting sprung doing exactly what she was doing now – puffing away madly – the only difference being that I did it in the girls' toilets.

Not that long ago I was dragged by the scruff of my neck into the principal's office yet again. The only discernible difference between this occasion and when I was hauled before the headmistress when I was a teenage student was that my daughter's headmistress did not have a cigarette in her hand.

The result of my maternal butterflies had been caught scribbling some very creative language in her creative language class.

Later that night, when my daughter returned home from school, I explained the facts of school life to my daughter. 'It is not OK to write naughty words in your schoolbook and leave them lying around for the headmistress to discover. For goodness sake, find a better hiding place next time.'

A few days later, I was called up to the school for another embarrassing, toe-curling experience.

My son was receiving the Honour Certificate for 'Displaying Very Responsible Behaviour.'

Later, I said to him, 'You do realise this is going to ruin my reputation.'

School reports

News flash! School reports that Bad Mother was a very bad student. 'Talks too much in class. Could try much harder.'

I was very trying at school. My teachers thought I was very trying as well. I tried my teachers' patience for all twelve years of my education. In fact, I tried so hard they gave me an extra two weeks holiday in my first year of high school.

Nowadays, my children are trying their teachers' patience. But that's OK. I'd be failing in my duty as a Bad Mother if my children weren't as trying as I was at school.

One end of term I got a good school report. My teachers were as surprised as I was. My parents were so surprised they bought me a big bar of Toblerone. I was so surprised that I stopped being so trying and settled down to try to learn something. What I learnt was that teachers were almost human. Not quite, but almost.

I was surprised, too, when I found out that learning was almost fun. Almost fun – let's not get carried away here.

My children are trying their hardest at school because if they don't I've threatened to put their size 10 uniform on my not size 10 body and sit next to them in school. Of course, I had the teachers' absolute approval on that one. That was when my three children threatened to take out a restraining order against me so I would not to come within 30 metres of their classroom.

Scare tactics work. I lost weight and nearly fitted into their size 10 uniform so I could scare some education into them.

I've always thought I wished I could go back to 1975 and know then what I know now. Wrong! If I had knowledge of what was to come – a real job, a mortgage, health insurance, having my own children, more trying school reports – I would have stayed in school for the rest of my life and become either a professional student or a teacher – well, same thing really.

Fifteen years after I left school the strangest thing happened. I went back to school and studied English literature and learnt what my teachers had tried to teach me all those years ago. I learnt that learning was fun, and the more I learnt the more I wanted to learn. I learnt, too, that learning was wasted on the young.

My children have encouraged my learning process. When I'm about to go out with the girls on a Saturday night, just as the taxi pulls up, my children yell after me, 'Don't get home too late Mum, you have homework to do tomorrow.'

School of rock

Just occasionally, I have to attend school functions whether I want to or not.

Just getting past the gates of my children's high school gives me a good dose of post-traumatic stress disorder and I remain in that hypervigilant state until I escape through the very same gates.

You can tell I went to a Catholic, all-girls' school, can't you?

I was prodded out of my post-lunch afternoon sleep and very reluctantly carted off to be part of the parent audience watching my son play the trombone in the high school's winter concert.

In my day, the only instrument ever to be heard within the

school grounds was the recorder, which I played, along with the rest of the band, in front of the primary school assembly – 'God Save the Queen', a tortuous rendition that had nothing to do with 1970s punk bands – or Molly Meldrum, or Freddie Mercury for that matter – and everything to do with Camilla Parker Bowles's current mother-in-law.

I doubt very much it's the number one song on Her Majesty's iPod, although I have a suspicion it might be one of Camilla's favourite songs, and the late Princess Diana's too.

You can take the girl out of England but you can't take England out of the girl and I can still toot that tune on the old recorder whenever the fancy takes me.

But recorders, like fusty, should-be-superannuated monarchies, are now just museum pieces. What happens in the music department at high schools these days is that teachers and adolescent kids now bond over drum kits and electric guitars. They have their own garage bands and they truly rock'n'roll.

It's a bit worrying when the teachers are *that* enthusiastic about their students. Having a good time at school was something that was actively discouraged back in the 1970s. I was taught everything I know by a group of fusty, superannuated nuns who, looking back over the years, I now realise they knew more about me than I did about myself. It's taken me nearly three decades to work out just how they knew – after years of teaching children, that's how they knew all about us.

It's because I'm an aetheist that it took me three decades to work that out.

Just to add, I'm not bitter and twisted because my sister got the piano lessons. Honestly. I'm not.

Growing old disgracefully

Recently, I was forced to attend, under duress, yet another school concert.

It never ceases to amaze me how my children's teachers are so adept at torturing innocent parents.

So I grumped along and sat moodily in my seat until the curtains were drawn. Despite myself, I ended up thoroughly enjoying all the dancing and singing.

I'd really like to know where those amazing, wonderful teachers gather up their passion and eagerness for life from. I want what they're having.

I have the flexibility of an ironing board when it comes to dancing and I'm the only person I know for whom The Birdie Dance has way too many complicated moves. I have an insane compulsion to dance and sing my way through menopause, when I should be home respectfully embroidering cushions and diligently knitting tea-cosies. I can't dance and I shouldn't sing.

But lack of singing talent has never stopped me from going to a pub and belting out some David Cassidy and Bay City Rollers songs, some Proclaimers and Savage Garden and putting the bricks and mortar into that all-time classic, 'Bob the Builder'. Just because I think I can sing doesn't mean I should open my mouth in public.

Karaoke was invented for frustrated singers who have far more enthusiasm than anything else going for them. If you're going to kiss and canoodle with your karaoke, make sure you're the loudest person in the pub, that your attending parents have a video camera and that they are hooked up to the internet.

Years ago, I took my children to the local church for the Christmas Karaoke Lunch. Naturally enough, I had absolutely no plans to get up and sing.

For the entire alcohol-free lunch, I couldn't stop thinking about what song I wasn't going to sing. Once the microphone was set up, though, I knew I was committed – either try or die in the attempt. None of my so-called friends would get up and sing with me, so I was on my own.

Well, not quite.

Halfway through the song I became vaguely aware of a tugging sensation on my right leg. I had become so carried away with myself that I hadn't realised that my then three-year-old son had wrapped himself around my leg and was screaming hysterically, which he continued to do for the duration of my performance.

Recently, I watched the very same son trick up a treat on the trombone and stomp up a storm during his rap dance routine, all thanks to some very dedicated teachers who believe in giving their students not so much an outcome-based education as an outcome-based life.

School holidays

There's only one thing worse than having the kids home on school holidays and that's having your husband take a week off work at the same time.

On Monday morning I'll heave a sigh of relief as I sit back and enjoy another depressing, violent and argument-filled episode of *EastEnders* in absolute peace and quiet. Albert Square must be permanently on school holidays.

On the positive side, school holidays mean never having to open the curtains, never having to change out of my pyjamas and being able to eat chocolate pancakes for breakfast, lunch and dinner, thereby saving on highly overrated, useless and expensive food items containing vitamins A, B, C, D and E.

I can also watch endless DVDs and fend off endless phone calls from the irate DVD shops requesting that overnight items please be returned the following day – not six weeks later. Our DVD overdue fine bill now exceeds our weekly alcohol bill.

Alcohol is more vital than oxygen when sitting through *American Pie* numbers 1, 2 and 3 with our son, a bunch of sniggering hormonal twelve-year-old boys and their scaly mates who wish their mothers and fathers would get the hell out of the house for the school holidays.

It's a bad sign when your kids have gone back to school and your ears are still ringing halfway through the next week. Organising a few friends over to your house for a midday session of orange juice heavily laced with Vitamin V for vodka always helps. The orange juice helps you with the hangover you're going to have to indulge yourself in the next day, and the vodka helps you to remember to forget to pick your children up after school.

Never underestimate the healing power of a bottle of mother's little helper laced with tales of your friends' own horrible children. It's gratifying to know there are worse-behaved brats than yours. Your friends have tales even your psychiatrist would shrink at.

If it wasn't for Bad Mothers, therapists would not be able to afford overseas holidays to exotic locations.

But it's the teachers who need therapy the most — anyone who wants to spend their waking hours with thirty little bast . . . I mean, darlings, definitely needs their head examined.

Spawn of Satan

One of the cheapest ways to entertain your children during the school holidays is to have other kids over. It transforms the whole atmosphere of the house. Usually, two's company and three's a testosterone-fuelled fist fight, but this time all the kids worked together making a movie.

They had all the necessary infrastructure — Lego and plasticine, a web cam, a digital camera and a mobile phone and ended up with something that gave Steven Spielberg a run for his money.

When they exhausted their film-making talents, they turned their attention to cricket, using some of my china ornaments as wickets. Yelling 'Howzat' at the top of their voices as my expensive hanging windchimes exploded gave me the opportunity to kick them outside into the sleet and snow.

We've only ever had one kid over that we really disliked. He had all the finesse and charm of a flesh-eating virus. Years ago, during a birthday party when it was pelting rain outside and I had a games room full of preschoolers to amuse with just several sheets of newspaper and three Freddo frogs, this Spawn of Satan disappeared somewhere within my house. I finally found him with his sticky fingers inside the goldfish tank, systematically flicking the fish out of the water. When he was done with that, he returned to the games room and proceeded to throw half a tonne of Lego over the floor.

Apparently, he didn't like party games and preferred to make his own fun. At last, I had found what I hadn't believed existed – a child more obnoxious than any of mine.

Somehow I managed to restrain myself from grabbing the front of his T-shirt and twisting it into a ball. Instead, between gritted teeth and only a few inches from his sulky face, I gently explained the facts of expected behaviour at a birthday party that did not involve fish flicking or Lego hurling antics.

A few days after the party I saw him at school weeing on the rosebushes in front of the headmaster's office, right in front of several mothers, including his own. Not discretely mind you, but waving it around like a high-pressure hose during a bushfire. In fact – and this is the best part – while the other mothers looked away, his mother gazed on indulgently.

It's always wonderful to see other boys behaving badly, especially if you can manage to get it all on digital camera. Watching it over and over again makes me feel as though I'm not doing such a bad job after all.

Camp as a row of tents

Camping is a great opportunity to bond with your children and to get in touch with nature.

But before embarking on our bonding and nature-filled school holiday we had to return overdue videos – plus pay fines, overdue library books – plus pay fines, overdue PlayStation games – plus fines, fill the petrol tank, get a prescription filled and pay the well-overdue (but luckily no fine) paper bill.

So we spent the first hour of our holiday driving around in

ever-decreasing circles until we finally broke free from the suburban whirlpool and headed off down the highway of life.

We subscribe to an internet camping forum that promotes the doctrine that the art of camping has more to do with how you pack – as well as what you pack.

Getting 10 tonnes of camping equipment into a space the size of a tissue box is the ultimate goal, apparently, rather than relaxing under the tarp with a good book and a glass of wine.

The portable television was left behind, disappointing my eleven-year-old son because it meant he was missing out on *Wifeswap*. And here I was thinking *Jerry Springer* was his favourite program.

Coca-Cola, lollies, three bored children and a long car journey is about as compatible with peace and harmony as former AFL player Sam Kekovitch is with rabid vegetarians, so, as we learnt years ago, ear plugs come in handy.

Despite our vigourous protests, my hubby decided that a shortcut was in order so we detoured onto a rocky dirt track.

Eventually, we arrived at our destination to a raging easterly breeze.

Windy in more ways than one, as it turned out. During the night (how can I put this delicately) nether-region bodily-function noises could be heard exploding, Chernobyl style, from senior-citizen-occupied caravans surrounding our tent, which made it very difficult to keep a straight face during the day when discussing with our temporary neighbours the various ways of blowing up the air mattresses.

The highlight of the trip for the adult contingent was the tour of the Pinnacles. We spent the majority of the time doubled over with laughter, pointing at the huge phallic-shaped rocks sticking out of the yellow sand.

On the way home we learnt the highlight of the children's trip was when a flock of birds flew over the river we had picnicked beside — several simultaneously dropped Christmas presents into the river, *Dambusters* style.

I knew then that the bonding with nature part of our trip had been a complete success.

Australian bush adventurer Russell Coight would be very proud of us.

Roman holidays

Road rage is currently the hippest rage around town. But what about the post-Christmas summer holiday rage that most mothers seem to suffer during the long, hot month of January?

Consensus among mothers is that the summer holidays are simply too long. Teachers, students and my three children seem to think otherwise. Which is why sending my children to their nanna's for the last week of the holidays is far more appealing than playing naked twister with Robbie Williams and Antonio Banderas.

They've spent the past five weeks in my face — my children that is — not Robbie or Antonio. Unfortunately.

Every time my children behaved grottily or used bad language I donated a dollar of their pocket money to the Tsunami appeal. Sorry kids, but 'focker', as in *Meet the Fockers*, is not an alternative swear word. Your pocket money has suddenly become tax deductible.

It was on the way to Nanna's that I experienced my first real road rage. The boys were shouting and messing around in the car and my daughter kept flicking the radio dial from my favourite station to hers.

So I screeched to a halt on the side of the road and raged at them that if they didn't behave themselves they would be spending not one week but two weeks at Nanna's. That shut them up quicker than you could say, 'Are we there yet?'

Just because I kicked the kids out the car in front of my parents' house without slowing down doesn't mean I haven't enjoyed the time we've spent together, and even though they were bugging me, we did manage to avoid taking out restraining orders against each other.

Their absence means I get to watch *Coronation Street* without thinking SpongeBob SquarePants has joined the revellers at the *Rover's Return*. That's the problem with having two televisions in the same house.

It also means my husband and I get to be newlyweds again and enjoy some quality time fighting over who does the dishes. We solved that problem by eating takeaway off the kitchen floor, *Nine and a Half Weeks* style.

Our children assumed that our private life ground to a halt once they were born and, for a while, they were right. But for five nights while they're away we don't have to close the bedroom door and pretend we are not doing anything other than sleeping.

So on Australia Day we set off our own fireworks – with a bit of morning glory – some afternoon delight and lots of midnight at the oasis – without having to explain our whereabouts to the children.

We now just have to explain away the food stains on the lino.

Take a walk on the wild side

Australia. Isn't that the continent where birds fly upside down? Where kangaroos hop down the street and the average garden backs onto a pristine golden beach? Where good neighbours become good friends and, if you're not careful, you'll get bitten on the bum by one of their dangerous and poisonous wildlife?

Our English relatives in the UK go into severe muscular spasms when you mention Australia's most dangerous and venomous wildlife. But that's OK, because we go into severe muscular spasms at the thought of our English relatives visiting the Land Down Under.

They've been known to inhabit the underside of toilet seats and bite unsuspecting bottoms as they crouch to do their business. Redback spiders that is, not our dreaded English relatives. Although I wouldn't put it past them.

The last batch were from Newcastle, England (but we'll forgive them for that) and on the very first night, my Aunt Patricia, whom I'd never met before, managed to mistake a tiny silverfish for an axe-wielding murderer.

Of all the places to be introduced to her first Antipodean creature, it was while enthroned upon the dunny hole (my boys' word for it, not mine), *aka* the loo or toilet.

Upon hearing a blood-curdling scream — and that was from the unfortunate silverfish — I kicked the toilet door open, Crocodile Dundee style, and was greeted by a vision that will haunt me for the rest of my natural life.

Knickers around her uplifted ankles and only halfway through her business, Aunt Patricia wanted me to get out my gun and shoot the bastard. I stepped on it instead and closed the door.

Now, I can never come across so much as a silverfish without thinking about auntie's size 22s dangling around her ankles.

My children, who had doubts about their English relatives even before they arrived in Western Australia, now had their worst fears confirmed. This was going to be a very long three weeks sleeping on rock-hard, smelly camp beds.

If Patricia had spotted a redback, we could've forgiven her, but we're talking about an insect that disintegrates into a cloud of silver dust if you so much as disturb the air around it.

Redbacks, on the other hand, have a much higher public profile. Redbacks normally live under toilet seats, garden chairs, sheds and fence capping – but not in trees. They have huge, black, shiny bodies with an iridescent red stripe on their back. Although numerous around the garden, they're quite shy and rarely jump out and attach themselves to your jugular vein. Some kids even take them to school in bug catchers, much to their teacher's delight.

There's another type of redback, which is brown, cold and wet, and native to pubs and clubs. If accidentally swallowed, it has a sharp bite. Symptoms include swaying, boasting, swearing, shouting, dizziness, blurred vision and vomiting; eventually you end up wishing you were dead.

Redback Beer is extremely common and the only antidote known to man is to drink more of it.

My friend Kylie (honest, that's her name) was walking down the Kiss and Drive Road at her kids' local school when something fell out of a tree and shot down her bra. To the utter amazement of the house-husbands picking up their offspring, Kylie ripped off her shirt and bra and jumped up and down screaming.

Kylie is a drop-dead, gorgeous blonde with tits to die for. One of the dads rushed up to her wondering if his luck had changed.

Unfortunately for him, a spider had the pleasure of biting Kylie's boobs first.

She was raced to the local hospital where a redback spider bite was diagnosed. By this stage she was dizzy and had black spots appearing before her eyes. As did half the dads at school, no doubt.

Later, she was explaining to her friend's husband that, in the absence of a spider body, the diagnosis for a redback bite is when the erectile hairs on the breasts don't flatten when pressed down. His response: 'You have hairy tits?'

The reptilian equivalent of the redback is the dugite snake. Until last Christmas, the only dugite, or any other snake for that matter, that I'd ever come across had been at our local zoo.

We spent Christmas Day camping down south in coastal Denmark with a bunch of multicultural backpackers, frying our brains out on beer and wine in the hot sun, and feasting on barbecued king prawns. By late evening we were as crisped as the prawns, and for the umpteenth time nature called my name.

As I approached the toilet block, I saw what I thought was a 4 centimetre-long brown thing slithering down the path towards the gap under the dunny-hole door. Assuming I was hallucinating from sunstroke – not the red wine of course – I dismissed it as an oversized legless lizard until my last remaining brain-cell kicked in and two things happened:

1 I realised it wasn't a 4 centimetre-long harmless, legless lizard
2 the only thing that was harmless and legless was me.

I grabbed a dustbin and chased the poisonous 2 metre-long brown dugite snake around the toilet block, determined to end my holiday with an intensive care hospital stay. Where's Steve Irwin when you need him?

Luckily, I wasn't coordinated enough to come close to scooping it up. The business end of the park owner's axe was rather more effective. Poor snake, he was just minding his own business when he lost his way (and his head).

The scariest part of this story is the fact that I just might have been dumb enough to attempt that sober. I made my children swear that they wouldn't tell this for news at school.

Bulk Rubbish-R-Us

Why buy expensive presents for your children when there is more fun to be had dragging home junk from the local bulk rubbish collection?

At first glance our street looks like delivery trucks from IKEA and Toys "R" Us have blown a tyre and strewn the contents across everyone's verge. But the fact is you could furnish a house with what other people have rejected: entire lounge suites, stereos, bookcases, fridges, stoves, washing machines. It would appear that a free television comes with every purchase as well.

There's a veritable smorgasbord of entertainment to be found on the side of the road. From the bulk rubbish people left for collection on the street, my two sons scavenged a pair of backless computer wheelie chairs. They've spent the best part of the school holidays whizzing around the back verandah, smashing into my plants and wrecking my garden beds, while their $300 telescope and $200 remote-controlled hovercraft lay languishing in their bedrooms. There's more low-cost fun to be had in our street at the moment than there is at the high-cost Perth Royal Show.

During the school holidays, they've brought home whipper-snippers, lawn mower parts, scooters with shonky brakes, two flat tyres and wobbly steering.

The amusement for them is pulling all the pieces apart and putting them back together to make one huge Frankenscooter with turbo engine, power steering and more grunt than a victorious Sydney Swans supporter at an AFL Grand Final.

My boys have no shame. And neither do I. While the rest of Perth enjoys the Royal Show, my kids have to forage through other people's rubbish. You'd be amazed at the amount of stuff on the side of the road you could fill a showbag with.

But the Nike is on the other foot when I've sprung other people rifling through my boxes of verge rubbish and I get really annoyed when they find something worthwhile. I want it back. I become the dog in the manger – I don't want the stuff but I don't want anyone else to have it either.

Like a fully loaded wheelie bin without the wheels, school holidays tend to drag on a bit. The bulk rubbish has been collected and now I have to find other ways to amuse the children on a shoestring budget. Hmmm, what's the address of the local rubbish tip?

6

Q: WHy IS IT so HARD TO save MONeY?

A: Debtors' Homes and Gardens

Money, money, money – never funny

Money is something I don't pay a lot of attention to – until it runs out. Money doesn't just burn a hole in my pocket, it sets fire to my entire wardrobe, which is why I have to spend so much money on clothes in the first place.

It's not that I'm simple-minded, but after spending $300 on seventeen items of heavily discounted, two sizes too small clothing at a bargain basement warehouse, I have to wonder about my emotional IQ level, especially after I told myself I'd diet my way into them. A year later, after gaining several kilos, I gave them to the Salvation Army. It's very easy to be dimwitted with hindsight.

Money can't buy you love, unless, of course, you are Richard Gere in *Pretty Woman*, but it can pay for my children's school fees and their clothes. Dressing my children leaves me and my purse light-headed. I could get away with department store clothes, even secondhand ones until they turned a certain age, but after that it was label clothing only.

Recently, we took out a loan so my daughter could buy a pair of $150 popular-label shorts. There was more material in an episode of *Home and Away* than in what actually covered her bum.

There are two types of people in this world. Those who can save and those who can't save to save their lives. Twenty years ago, when I got married, I brought into our union a fifteen-year-old, mustard-coloured Datsun 180B, a credit card debt and several suitcases of emotional baggage.

My husband brought with him a large savings account and a very brief briefcase. The only emotional baggage he had was what he would acquire from what I was about to dish out over the next two decades.

Back in the 1980s, budgeting was about living on tomato sauce sandwiches so I could afford to catch a bus to work so I could afford to eat tomato sauce sandwiches. I managed to stay on target because back then credit cards, unless you were super rich and therefore didn't need one, hadn't yet been invented for people with no cash. But the sole reason we need credit in the first place is because we don't have enough money to live beyond our means.

No matter how much money we earned – and even the filthy rich live up to their pay packets every week – budgeting bore as much reality to our lives as insider trading rules did to the wealthy and the wicked.

If you think money doesn't make the world go round, just try saving up for an extended overseas holiday. Packing twice as much money, half as many clothes and all of your credit cards will still leave you short and gasping about a third of the way through your dream trip.

Holidaying in London and Paris, there are some things I just can't live without. But what's the point of buying a Chanel handbag if I only have fifty cents to put in it? Having cold hard cash in my hand is much more thrilling than anything it could possibly buy. The only time I've been well and truly stinking rich is when I owned two hotels on Park Lane and Mayfair and had seven thousand monopoly dollars in the bank.

If you order a cheap salad for lunch, it's better to let people think you are on a diet and full of will power rather than that you are broke. That will show the rest of the world that you have style, class, taste and of course money.

The easiest way to make a small fortune is to start with a big one – and have three children. If I counted my wealth in children I would be rich beyond my wildest dreams, but I'd still have very little money in the bank. There's nothing like a teenager to empty your wallet quicker than a politician with an expense account.

There are lots of things I can do that don't cost money. Sweating, sleeping, taking the dog for a walk. Even breathing doesn't cost money. Yet. Although I'm sure a future government will think of a way to tax us on fresh air.

I am appalled when I think of the money I have wasted over the years. If I had a dollar for every dollar I've wasted I'd be a multimillionaire.

Money doesn't buy you happiness so much as it purchases less anxiety in life. That's where an angst-reducing chequebook comes in handy. That way you can send the electricity bill to the gas company and vice versa. When the cheques come back send them to the right utility, but forget to sign them. That will tide you over until next month's pay when you can start the whole confusing process over again. The beauty is, if the cheque does end up bouncing, it's the other party that ends up out of pocket, not you. Robbing Visa to pay Mastercard is also a legitimate means of staving off the snarling debt collector from one's door.

I used to get excited about the end of financial year tax cheque. It took me many years to realise that I wasn't actually being given a bonus by a benevolent government. It was my money to begin with.

Exercise and fresh air can cost you nothing if you are smart. So I signed up with the local hot, sweaty and airless gym and expended more energy agonising over not going than if I actually went there on a regular basis and worked out.

The less exercise I did the more money it cost me. I didn't learn my lesson, either. So far in my life, I've done that three times. My husband's done it only once.

It would be a good idea to get some regular exercise as we need to live wiser and healthier – so we can extend our mortgage every few years.

I'd love to live the Lotto dream, only right at this very moment I simply can't even afford to buy the winning ticket.

Wasted money

I shop with the passion and zest that only the truly addicted can understand. If I counted up all the money I've wasted over the years I would just sit down and cry.

Life is full of bitter disappointment and endless frustration. If you're lucky, you will finally find an overpriced pair of jeans that fits perfectly. I'm yet to find the perfect-fitting pair of jeans.

Just as disappointing, as frustrating and expensive is the price of petrol. So why am I still driving the kids to school? Because it takes a lot more than rising petrol prices to wake me out of my complacency and what convoluted quirk of fate decreed that bottled water would cost more per litre than petrol? Just as well our car doesn't run on water. If it did, we wouldn't be able to afford it.

Aside from wasting money buying petrol and the odd bottle of water, our other favourite waste of the folding stuff is paying exorbitant fines for overdue videos, which are closely followed by overdue library book fines. Why? Because we are bone lazy when it comes to returning books and videos, that's why.

It's very easy for the family wallet to continually haemorrhage money when you have three kids. Buying a cricket set for the boys seemed doomed to success, until one of our sons left the ball out in the rain and it ended with more splits in it than an acrobatic team.

One day he came home with a smashed finger. I took one look at it and screamed, 'Oh, my God. Your fingernails are filthy', after which I wrapped a packet of frozen peas around his finger and gave him a Panadol. Much cheaper than a bunch of X-rays and an emergency department bill. Well, really, there's no sense wasting money and it saves me the embarrassment of other people having to view his grotty fingernails.

One of the cheapest ways to entertain the family is to watch family videos. The good part is the fact that there will never be any overdue fines on these videos. The bad part is that you will have to explain to the third child why he doesn't appear as often as his older brother and sister.

My two sons and my daughter are all not speaking to me this week. That's OK with me because, not only is life a lot quieter, but it's also considerably less expensive.

I'm off to the shops now to look for that elusive pair of jeans. But, like family harmony in the suburbs, finding them could be just one big illusion.

My Virgin credit card is a slut

Lack of money is the root of all evil. That's why credit cards were invented.

Having a credit card addiction is a bit like suffering from Alzheimer's disease. You forget where you are, or why you're using it in the first place and eventually go into complete denial when confronted by your other half.

It's all about that intoxicating adrenaline rush that occurs when your card is swiped. Like text messaging with one hand, it's almost as good as sex.

After melting the plastic, or the keys on your mobile phone pad, you're walking on air as you head off for a post-climactic lunch. Paid for, of course, by your ever-faithful credit card.

It would appear that most men are immune to credit card euphoria, unless of course they're shopping at Bunnings or Mitre 10.

My Virgin credit card has become an insatiable slut. I get a constant stream of letters from banks and financial institutions outrageously flirting and trying to seduce me into selling my soul to the devil.

The problem with credit card application forms is that you have to prove you don't need the money before the bank is willing to lend you any.

Credit is wonderful if you can afford to pay back the

monthly bills, but if I lived within my budget my life would be tedious.

Just like sweets at the supermarket checkout point, placed there for unwary mothers, almost unlimited credit at almost zero interest rates is right in my face when I am at my most vulnerable – which is most of the time.

The only thing that remains consistent in my life is our level of debt and the persistent squawks of my three children begging for money at the weekends. I sense a correlation between those two.

Maybe I should attend a counselling group that deals with addiction. There's lots of help available and the beauty is, you can pay the fees off in installments with your credit card.

It's time now to be master of my own card and start practising safe sex with Richard Branson.

Budget book at bargain basement price: $2

Lead pencil: 50 cents

Ability to control impulses, delay gratification and freedom from credit card debt: priceless

There are some things that money can't buy, and for everything else – there's a weekly spending plan severely limited by hard-earned cash.

All mothers are working mothers

I spent the best part of the 1990s breastfeeding and seeing life through the eyes of Oprah Winfrey and Phil Donohue and their guests. When I started to regard them as all-knowing gurus, I knew it was time to go back to work.

I was amazed that I was looking forward to going back to work. I had vowed never to return to paid employment once I had had children, but after ten years as a stay-at-home mum, I was excited and raring to go – more fool me. The money helped, although having to fork out for petrol, clothes and lunches made a considerable dent in the pay packet.

Like all working mothers, I now had two full-time jobs. It was quite scary, but we quickly got used to having the extra money and wondered how we ever managed without it.

When the slave trade ended, they opened up call centres to replace it. The basic requirement in procuring the job in a call centre was to have suffered at least one nervous breakdown and be threatening to have another one in the very near future. Luckily, I managed to qualify on both counts.

Eight to eight became the new nine to five. Management had finally woken up to the fact that there were at least another four hours of the working day they had previously failed to exploit. But bosses of call centres are not all complete mongrels. Most of them are incomplete ones lacking in foresight, compassion and a sense of humour.

They take their jobs seriously. Very seriously. Most of them spend their day goose-stepping around the office making sure you are not putting on lip balm, brushing your hair, stretching your legs or ringing your therapist. Their job is to make sure you are doing your job.

All call centres are the same and management would prefer it if employees did not have annoying bodily functions.

Timed toilet breaks are the norm. My suggestion that we sit on commodes and shackle ourselves to our desks and each other was a serious item placed high on the agenda at the staff meeting. But at the meeting a motion was passed that perhaps corks might be more cost-effective.

One September weekend I was home long enough to empty my children's schoolbags only to find newsletters dating back to April and Mother's Day cards dating back to May. I grabbed my pillow, shoved it over my face and cried. By this stage, I'd been working for six months and had virtually forgotten what my children looked like and couldn't remember where their school was located.

Alcohol and antidepressants, the Stepford pills of life, quell the conscience of even the most angst and anxiety ridden good, bad or indifferent working mother. I'm amazed the medication trolley isn't wheeled down the aisles of Call Centre Battery Farm twice a day.

'Tea, Mrs Bad Mother?'

'Yes, please. White with two Prozac.'

I've often thought that, if I collapsed at my desk, management would replace me before calling the ambulance.

Next time you're waiting on the other end of the phone, please – *please* – remember, your call is not only a complete nuisance to us, but we'd also actually like you to just bugger off and leave us in peace.

Bitter homes and gardens I – No compromise!

A few years ago, we made the biggest mistake of our lives, aside from becoming parents that is. We decided that light-coloured carpets and walls was a compatible combination with three toddlers.

That was back in the vintage 1980s when the only two colours that mattered were beige and mission-brown. After due consideration it has been universally decreed that mission brown is not so much a colour as the biggest decorating blunder ever.

Beige is now euphemistically referred to as 'fawn' or 'camel' or 'ivory'. But a rose by any other name is still beige. As Billy Connolly is reputed to have said, 'Beige is ordinary and dull and belongs to boring people in immaculate blazers.'

Pretty much the same as the discovery that boring women have immaculate homes. I have a friend who keeps her vacuum cleaner next to the door so that when she has unexpected visitors, she can cover herself by saying she was just about to tidy up and vacuum.

Which, of course, is the greatest piece of codswallop since Madonna said she was tired of being a Legendary Rock Icon and just wanted to cook, iron and dust for her new husband instead.

I dust our house every six months whether it needs it or not. But the hardest job of all is agreeing how to drag our house into the new millennium. At the moment there are so many disagreements that we are going around in circles and I'm in danger of disappearing up my own argument.

Painting the house, for instance. We booked ourselves into Bunnings and spent an hour watching different types of paint dry.

But, unlike watching lifestyle programs on television, or live out-takes at Bunnings, doing it yourself is never as much fun as watching someone else do it for you.

Trouble is – do-it-yourself lifestyle programs bear no resemblance to reality.

Just because the IKEA catalogue is the world's second most distributed publication doesn't mean you should try assembling one of their products at home. Putting together the fifty-five requisite pieces of a bookcase that comes with dodgy pidgin English instructions is not my definition of retail therapy.

Physical violence has been known to occur in our household. That's what happened after spending six hours on Christmas Eve putting together the 5000 pieces of Barbie's Mobile Home for my then four-year-old daughter, which is why, until they have free marriage counselling sessions at IKEA, we will never, ever shop there again.

Never compromise on paint colour, or husbands, because only one of you will end up satisfied. Let your wife win, because if your wife's happy then the rest of the family will be suffering a whole lot less.

Bitter homes and gardens 2 – Can you keep kids and a garden?

We live in a suburb where cocos palms were the height of fashion twenty years ago. There seemed to be a competition to see just how many cocos palms would fit on a quarter-acre block. Our neighbours won – thank goodness.

Two decades on, several mission-brown houses are now almost completely obscured by endless rows of cocos palms.

Not that there's anything wrong with that — it's just that there isn't anything right with it either. As far as we're concerned, the only good cocos palm is a dead cocos palm.

Cocos palms, like weeds and small children, seem to thrive on neglect. There are gardens in our street that permanently remain immaculate with no visible effort from the occupants.

Ours is not one of those houses, but only because the cocos palms are greener on the other side of the fence. Colour me mission brown, but it would appear our garden is a desert in the middle of a cocos palm-lined oasis.

The grass that grows in our flower beds is greener than the grass we call a lawn and I'm sure our family could kill even Astroturf with kindness if we tried hard enough.

Our Geraldton wax seems to wane more than it waxes. But — correct me if I am wrong —isn't the whole idea of gardening to have plants that actually grow bigger rather than appear to shrink in size?

Every time I look at my kumquat trees there are more leaves on the ground than there are on the actual trees, which has nothing to do with the fact that the kids use the trees as stumps for cricket. Does it?

Letting kids loose in the garden is a great idea if you plan on heavily supervising them, or using this banishment as a time-honoured punishment.

So I let the kids loose to see what wondrous magic they could spread like dog and cat fertiliser over the garden. It wasn't like it could get any worse and it would give them something to do other than watching television or text messaging the kids next door.

All the while I sat back, supervised them while holding a glass of wine in my hand and generally sat around watching the grass grow in places that it shouldn't.

The boys had decided self-sufficiency reigned supreme and committed themselves to spinach, broccoli and tomatoes.

My teenage daughter decreed it was her job to simply wander aimlessly around the garden while looking very pretty, something she excelled at. Because her boyfriend now spends more time at our house than his, we've had to add him to the jobs roster as well.

It was as I sat watching the kids that I realised the threat of sending them out to garden as a punishment was no longer a viable option.

My kids were having way too much fun for that.

Smells like teenage socks

Boys smell. Little boys have their own special afterschool summer stink, a mixture of sweaty jocks sandwiched between a bum and a hard place all day and sweaty, grotty socks and sneakers that emit their own personal whiff factor.

Just ask any harassed mother who does the school run in an unairconditioned car.

Big boys also stink – in their own, very special, very different way. It's the little boy afterschool summer stench with the added bonus of blossoming testosterone.

Only mozzarella toe-jam can rival the pungency of a Boy Scout's underpants after a week of remote bushland camping. Real Boy Scouts change their socks and undies once a month, whether they need to or not.

My boys' bedrooms, while reasonably tidy, manage to consistently smell salty and piquant. No amount of air freshener can get rid of that teenage dirtbag man smell.

On the other hand, my daughter's personal space smells of rose-scented incense but resembles a train wreck. I'm constantly incensed at the state of her bedroom.

Worse than the aromatic bouquet of dead and dying socks is the quantum physics law I call 'the black hole factor' in our washing machine that constantly eats only odd socks. The even socks get sucked into the writhing maelstrom concealed beneath our washing machine and appear with a slurp through the Stargate into our back garden. All of them mud-starched to stiff upper lip perfection.

After Stargate, our dog is the next prime suspect and she smells much sweeter than the socks she allegedly steals.

My youngest son wears the same tinea-ridden socks day in, day out; my daughter hides hers and then complains she has none to wear.

My Boy Scout son throws his against a wall. If they stick they need washing, if they fall down he gets another week-long camp out of them.

My husband's not much better. He leaves a trail of peeled off, sweaty, black socks in his wake, a bit like Hansel and Gretel's breadcrumb trail and, just like Hansel and Gretel, my husband finds a snarling, evil witch at the end of the trail waiting to devour him.

But the winner of the Sad Sack Scary Sock Competition goes to someone who shall remain nameless.

He has rows and rows of sweet-smelling identical socks — all mathematically t-squared into rigid submission. So alike you couldn't pick one out in an identity parade.

I actually saw Hannibal Lector's mother inside his sock drawer. Now that's enough to scare the socks off of anybody.

Ironing the creases out of life

Peace of mind is being able to meditate in the middle of the supermarket where not only your children scream at you, but the products on the shelves do also.

You don't need to sit on top of a snow-covered mountain to find harmony and fulfilment. Sit on a mountain of ironing instead. Turn on, tune in and zone out while effortlessly ironing fifty-five pairs of jocks and socks.

Get in touch with your inner child. Behind every man watching the Brownlow medal awards there's a twelve-year-old boy wanting to kick the winning goal.

Practice random acts of laughter inside your house. If you ever wanted to do your kids' heads in, that's the way to do it. They'll accuse you of going crazy but you know that you are slowly going completely sane.

Do it for long enough and your teenagers will practice random acts of cleaning and caring. They won't have a clue as to why they have this overwhelming urge to do so, they'll just feel compelled to do it. They'll think the sun shines out of your rear end and honour you by tidying up their bedrooms.

Meditating makes you happy. I went along to my children's sports day and found myself cheering madly at the tunnelball games and when they played *Chariots of Fire* over the running races – it was all I could do not to get up and break the record for the four minute mile myself.

The black spots in the shower don't matter as much as the clean spots in your brain. Once you realise that, you can then give your children peace of mind rather than a piece of your mind. Get in touch with your Mother. Mother Nature, that is. She won't run her white glove over your precious ornaments when she visits, she'll run Mr Sheen over the furniture for you instead.

I used to think I suffered from postnatal depression and the early onset of Alzheimer's disease, but it turned out to be nothing more than a lack of peace of mind. Once I realised that, it was time to don my Supermum outfit and get in touch with my inner ironing pile.

Sometimes, reality is an illusion caused by children.

7

Q: DO YOU ever FeeL as Though you are FaKING YOUR LIFe?

A: Guilt Magnets-R-Us

Faking it

It's been said that if you can fake genuine sincerity, you've got it made. I have to admit to making it up as I go along.

Nothing in my life is planned: it just seems to happen and I tag along. My conspiracy theory is that someone else is living my perfect life in a parallel universe.

The meaninglessness of some of the most unpalatable truths of everyday life comes down to just one question: Does my bum looks big in a pair of denim Levis? If you have to ask, chances are the answer is yes.

I faked it in the bedroom recently. I told someone that my bedsheets were from the Laura Ashley Collection, not K-Mart's generic brand, which is what they really were.

Faking a life has everything to do with covering up bizarre and naked truths. Who hasn't been in the middle of a blazing domestic when the phone rings or someone knocks on the door, and both you and your partner speedily retrovert into Mike and Carol Brady?

Some parts of my life are so downright ugly that I have to pinch myself to get to sleep. Rather than spend Sunday settling back in front of the fire with a *Will and Grace* marathon on television and a big box of chocolates, I told my boys that yes, of course I'd like to go for a long walk around Lake Monger in the pouring rain with their remote controlled hovercraft.

Or at least it would have been a long walk if my son's mobile phone hadn't dropped out of his pocket. After backtracking and eventually locating his phone I took him home and along with his brother gave him a sound thrashing – at Monopoly. In front of the fire. Watching a *Will and Grace* marathon. With a huge box of chocolates on the couch next to me.

Every Monday morning, without fail, I have children feigning sickness, begging me not to send them to school. While they pretend to be sick, I pretend to be concerned as I push them out the door, schoolbag firmly strapped to their backs.

Once the kids are out of the way, I can finally alter my own ego, thanks to Revlon. As I trowel on the make-up, I discover I can fit more foundation on my face that in the concrete footings of a highrise building where the Sopranos bury their bodies. Afterwards, I could well be in a witness relocation program; no one who knows me would recognise me.

I can't imagine skinny people bothering to weigh themselves more than once in a lifetime, but when I jump on the scales, they cry out in pain and implore me to lose at least 5 kilos. I'll deny the extra weight of course – denial and faking it are country cousins – then argue with the inert machine.

Have you ever seen a mature person squabble with a set of bathroom scales before tossing them out the window?

To keep my weight down, I become The Faked Chef. Instead of lamb-fatted roast spuds, I'll put frozen, steamed potatoes on the table and pass them off as fresh.

What do you mean, this tastes like soggy water? I've been slaving over a hot microwave all afternoon and just because the pavlova came in a box marked 'The Cheesecake Shop' doesn't mean I can't whip up a batch of hysteria all by myself.

If I can fake my own cucumber and carrot, then it's possible to fake anything. I know someone who is always terracotta-tanned in summer and a delicate shade of peaches and cream in winter. Considering she's well over the half-century mark, it's almost a supernatural manifestation.

Finally, it occurred to me that something was rotten in the State of Denial. Colour me Coppertone, but she had me completely bamboozled. Until I realised that, like the cast and crew of Baywatch, she was faking her own suntan.

If Australia can fake its bronzed buff then perhaps the Americans could fabricate a fraudulent moon-landing after all. The movie, *Capricorn One*, purported that America had landed itself on Mars in the 1980s. It starred a certain O J Simpson, who has convinced himself that the truth is still out there, it's just that he hasn't found the right evidence. Yet.

Living in denial of murderous intentions! Lies, deceit and double-crossings! Suspicious paranoid behaviour! Not just another celebrity murder trial or the latest edition of Big Brother Uncut, but what happens in this house when the last piece of pavlova is pilfered from the fridge.

Luckily, heavy make-up is hiding my red face as I discreetly brush the crumbs off my jumper.

Unplugged

There is a secret society of women who have discovered there's more to life than getting their lazy teenage daughters to tidy their rooms, or their procrastinating husbands to change the washer on that dripping tap. Who recognise that there's more to Me Time than getting up early to sweat it out to *Aerobics Oz Style*.

All harassed, overworked and underpaid mothers should be let in on this secret, the one that stops targetless anger threatening the harmony of the family, that makes mother feel good, gives her a healthy inner glow and even promotes weight loss.

Have you guessed it yet? Well, here's a clue. Once you've outlaid the money for some decent hardware, it'll cost you virtually nothing for the rest of your life – except for the price of the batteries.

Owning one's own pleasure machine is not what housewives or mothers generally talk about. It's a little secret we keep to ourselves, revealed only to our closest friends after a few drinks on a girls' night out.

It's like owning a pair of crotchless knickers. Everyone thinks they're tacky, but lots of us have some hidden in our drawers.

How do I know? I found out at a Tupperware party at which no one actually bought anything. In fact, once we discovered one of us owned a long, cylindrical power tool that wasn't used to bolt two pieces of wood together, plastic food containers moved quickly off the agenda. Suddenly, we were divided into two camps: The Girls Who Have and The Girls Who Haven't.

The Girls Who Have convey a coded message to each other, and it's not a secret handshake either – more like a raised eyebrow, a sideways smirk and a brief nod. It's not hard to persuade the Girls Who Haven't to become the Girls Who Have. All it takes is a visit to the shop with black windows.

Buying one is probably the most embarrassing experience you'll go through, until your teenage son finds it under the bed. People who make a living cleaning carpets have to move everything to get the job done properly. Guess what's the most common item found under Australian beds?

I've been to one of those black window places – the architectural equivalent of a pimpmobile – and seen some things that can best be described as mind-blowing.

I wandered around these surreal displays with my shades on, hoping to God I didn't run into someone I knew, terrified that one of my old school friends would be behind the counter, and ask, 'Would you like to try that, Madam?'

Of course, there's mail order or the internet, but then you don't have the option of trying before you buy, of handling the merchandise, so to speak. Remember, you always get what you pay for.

Personally, I believe nothing under $200 is really worth the effort and two speeds and two rotating controls is about the minimum you want. Anything less than that and you may as well have sex with your husband.

Having got it home, you'll zip through the washing, ironing – frigging everything – in record time, just so you can go play with your favourite pet. It doesn't demand equal rights in the bedroom and can't count to sixty-nine. The pleasure is all yours. It takes all the hard, sweaty work out of having to please someone else.

Take it from me, it's impossible not to climb the highest mountain when you have your hands wrapped round the best equipment in the world. You don't have to fake your own fireworks either. Satisfaction guaranteed. The only thing you'll ever have to fake again is a headache on Saturday night, when the girls want to take you out drinking. You'll already have a previous engagement – upstairs, at home.

Forget yoga and Pilates. Have your own personal workout at home. In front of the video. What better way to relax after a hard morning's housework than shagging the favourite movie star of your mind? Afterwards, why not have a post-climactic smoke on the patio? None of your neighbours will be any the wiser, unless you left the curtains or front door open.

Call it a hobby if you like. It beats sewing curtains, doing pottery classes or ironing thirty-five shirts to creaseless perfection. When hubby comes home at the end of the day and asks what you have been doing all day, you can just say you've been busy discovering the inner you.

And as we all know, if Mum's happy, then the rest of the family is too. Or at least, they're not suffering as much as usual.

You can do it anytime, anywhere, only do remember to take the batteries out when flying overseas; if you don't, you risk being hauled off the airplane in a foreign country to answer some very embarrassing questions.

Remember that Cyndi Lauper song, 'She Bop'? It was all about heading south to the danger zone, and I'm not talking Margaret River. I didn't discover the rapturous pleasures of 'She Bop' until I was twenty-one. I suffered many a frustrated night knowing I was missing out on something wonderful, but not knowing what that something wonderful was. It took a porno movie and an afternoon's journey of self-discovery to find out just what it was. After that, having actual sex was more of a damp squib than the Australia Day SkyShow. But I still didn't realise why multipacks of batteries are sold at checkout points and it was still some time before I furtively visited the black window shop to look for things I hadn't known existed.

Later on in life, when I heard such things did exist, I didn't want anyone to think I was sad and lonely, so I was forty-one, the age of liberation, where one doesn't give a rat's arse what other people think, before I discovered that a 'rabbit' didn't always mean a small, furry animal.

Could it make men redundant? Certainly, if the government put a tax on the number of southern sneezes we have there'd be enough money to fund a full-time ironing man for every working and every stay-at-home mother in the land.

There's no need to feel guilty – but you will. It goes with the territory. Just never let on to your other half just how addicted you've become to his rival. If you have to tell him, colour your conversations with stories about rabbits, polar bears and mountain lions and let him think you've subscribed to the *National Geographic* channel.

The best part is, you can't get pregnant or catch some awful communicable disease. You can be as loud or as quiet as you like and get to do what rabbits are best at – multiplication – until the kids come home from school to discover that Mum is in a good mood – at last.

Sex might be great, but there's no substitute for the Real Thing.

Naughty but nice

Is it any wonder that we fortysomethings are sexually confused?

In my childhood, I was a devotee of Milly-Molly-Mandy, who was always attending parties; I thought it was Pass the

Parcel and Musical Chairs she enjoyed, but let me read you an excerpt.

'Once upon a time, as Milly-Molly-Mandy was going to school, she noticed a number of young men come striding along from the crossroads and up Hooker's Hill.'

What a floozy! What a trollop, a strumpet!

Because I have lived my life wearing rose-coloured glasses, I didn't realise that Milly-Molly-Mandy, like that homosexual couple Big Ears and Noddy, were not the product of sweet minds, but the handiwork of wild, wanton women with nothing but unbridled passion throbbing in their veins.

Otherwise, how else could we explain away the writings of, say, that sexually repressed author, Enid Blyton, and her characters Cousin Dick and Aunt Fanny and the poor, tormented Uncle Quentin who had a voracious proclivity towards spanking young, unruly children?

Children's stories are about as politically correct as giving your child a publicly administered backhander – even if it is well-deserved.

While children's books are full of 'innocent innuendoes', what about all those overtly smutty 1970s television shows? Take the *Brady Bunch*, for instance. Who could sit still after witnessing all that sexual tension between Marcia and Greg? And what about Alice the housekeeper? With Sam the Butcher slipping her the meat every other episode, no wonder she was always so pleasant and jolly.

Even the Skipper and Gilligan couldn't keep their hands off each other. And why did Gilligan always sleep on top?

Did you ever wonder why the sexless professor always sublimated his libido by constantly knocking out radio-transmitter technology with a pair of coconuts? He never did get

Mary-Anne's subtle hints when she used to wave her coconut cream pies in his face. In fact, most of the time he used to leave them sitting untouched on the dinner table. It wasn't only Mr and Mrs Howell who weren't having sex on that particular island.

There was about as much subtlety to the 1970s as there was to Mrs Slocombe's pussy.

And while we're being naughty – but nice – let's time-warp into the twenty-first century. We have tickets to see a rugby game soon, so to get myself into the mood I watched a game on television. What I saw wasn't so much a rugby game but a frenzy of homoerotic foreplay by attractive men in loose-fitting boxer shorts chasing an oval piece of pigskin around a muddy field, that is, when they weren't scrumming across the grass locked together in an orgy reminiscent of the movie *Caligula*. That certainly smacked the rose-coloured glasses off my face.

Perhaps C3PO is gay after all.

8

Q: why DO I GET SUCH PLEASURABLE FEELINGS FROM CHRONIC SELF-INDULGENCE?

A: Seven Deadly Sins

Consumed by envy

Envy was one of my childhood friends because I had no one else to compare with. An only child, Mum and Dad provided me with a sibling, finally, when I was nine. At last, someone lower than me in the family pecking order to persecute and oppress so I could feel better about myself. And I did.

Even though I was the oldest child, I suffered from Middle Child Syndrome, believing, rightly or wrongly, that my younger sister received the lion's share of our parents' attention. I loved my sister dearly, but it was a clear case of Marcia, Marcia, Marcia.

I never had the confidence to admit I was envious of my sister. That would have been like admitting to suffering cowardice, guilt, shame and anger, dishonourable qualities in anyone. But when you don't like who you are, you always want what the other person has, until, in time, your envy consumes you, takes over your life and, finally, you end up in some sort of therapy.

I envied people with large families. At a recent school reunion my friend with a very large family admitted to envying me for being an only child. Her mother and father had to divide their precious spare time between seven children whereas I had Mum and Dad all to myself until I was nine, which, looking back on it, is probably why I ended up in therapy in the first place.

It's my job to sift through therapy and put together all the resonating nuggets of wisdom. Ninety per cent of therapy I do by myself at home. It took me the best part of ten years to realise that the other man's weeds are just as green on his side of the fence.

Suffering from envy is like having a wound that never heals, like ripping off scabs and having a good poke around, which was my favourite pastime. I was too terrified to let anything heal over. There's nothing quite like the painful pleasure of wallowing in your own misery.

Many years ago friends of friends won a huge amount of money in the lottery. I was murderously jealous of them. They now had enough money to emotionally sustain them through life. Two years later they were divorced, the money squandered and they were left far worse off than before their win.

I learnt from my daughter, my sister, even the friends of friends, the importance of being an original and that envy is not necessarily a predisposed one-way trip to hell. It's not whether you inevitably suffer envy, but how you handle it that matters.

Both my daughter and my sister own their individuality and wear it as a badge of honour. They are the copied – they are not the facsimile.

Envy often manifests itself as a malignant praise, a compliment gone wrong. But to be without envy, is to be without life. Only the dead can't envy.

Lust while you dust

Sex. No, not the number between five and seven spoken in Kiwi, but the main, if not the entire, incentive for the survival of the human species. Life is what happens in between bouts of scorching, raunchy sex, not the other way around.

According to the Catholic church, 'Lust is disordered desire for or inordinate enjoyment of sexual pleasure', and 'Anyone who looks at another lustfully has already committed adultery with her in his heart.'

Apparently, according to church dogma, women do not feel this crazy little thing called lust. Someone try telling that to my libido.

It's not as if I think the Catholic church is out of step with the rest of us lecherous heathens, it's just that I spent a disproportionate amount of upper school time hiding in classroom cupboards, fantasising about Leif Garrett and Shaun Cassidy, in order to escape mass.

Between the ages of thirteen and twenty-five I used to get aching pangs of hungry, animalistic desire every other waking moment. The cure for lust would appear to be marriage.

After twenty years of marriage, give me a good book and a cup of hot sex any day. I am not ashamed to say that I am as guilty as sin when it comes to disordered desires.

Just sitting on the beach watching the hot young bods jog across my line of vision when I'm watching my children try not to drown themselves is enough to get my fervid imagination running riot.

It's not my fault I'm a dirty old woman. God made me this way. My body might be a bit past its use-by date, but my mouth is watering, I'm getting breathless and blushing, and I'm thinking I can sort of see how Mrs Robinson got herself into trouble in the first place. When I get these hot flushes all over my body, I'm not sure if it's because I'm rapidly approaching menopause or whether I'm just tuning into my inner Anne Bancroft.

At my age and status in life, I should be repressing my desire and channelling my sensuality into cleaning out cupboards and allowing my hair to grow a fetching shade of iron grey. I should be getting my biggest thrills knitting tea-cosies, sitting on committees and judging the jam section at the local show rather than hankering after men half my age at pubs and nightclubs.

If I carry on at this rate, according to the pontificating Pope, I'll be languishing in purgatory forever. But at least I'll have most of my mates and a few horny young devils to keep me company.

It's not as though I'm treading untrodden ground. Men have been hunting nubile young flesh since time began. While we women were barefoot and pregnant in the caves, the men in our lives were night-clubbing young girls over the head. The more things change, the more they stay the same.

When men do this, they're following the natural order of things. When women do it, it's considered to be a very unnatural display of unladylike behaviour. But hey, I've never been accused of ladylike behaviour in my entire life.

I have a confession to make about when I'm indulging in a bit of the old primitive frumpy-rumpy-pumpy. Sometimes it's not my husband I am thinking about. Sometimes I'm thinking about whether the electricity bill got paid last week. Did I remember to record *Law and Order SVU*? Hang on a minute, darling, let me check the video. If I'm not back in two minutes, start without me.

Lust is guaranteed to get you into trouble. Keanu Reeves used to be number one on my lust list, until I discovered Robbie Williams, my current favourite drenched and dripping wet dream. Oh yes, women can have wet dreams too, and it's not the dirty dish water that's drenching us. It's the dirty look on Robbie Williams's face.

It's a bit off-putting when you can't take a raunchy romp in the sheets because your teenage children don't go to sleep until well after your bedtime. Taking precautions at our age means closing the bedroom door so the kids can't hear. There is nothing more ridiculous-looking than two people engaged in the horizontal mambo.

There's only one thing that makes your flesh crawl more than the thought of your parents swinging from the chandelier and that's when you know your teenage children are thinking about hanging off the light globes as well.

Angry antics

Aside from lust, anger, another of the other Seven Deadly Sins, is probably the next most seductive. Who hasn't been seduced by the dark side of the force? Who hasn't given in to their anger?

According to Aristotle, anybody can become angry, that is easy; but to be angry with the right person, and to the right degree, and at the right time, and for the right purpose, and in the right way, that is not within everybody's power. That is not easy.

I've been accused of arrogant self-righteous anger before, as well as most of the other seven deadly sins, but that was by family members who don't count anyway. I'd rather be neurotic than stonkingly boring; just ask my husband and children.

I've spent many an exhilarating and impotent hour plotting revenge against various people, twisting and turning my grievances inside out, licking my wounds and anticipating the bitter confrontations to come. I now just have to sit down and wait until my husband and children get home.

One of the most pointless arguments my husband and I had was how many T-shirts I should pack for a Bali holiday; it ended in fisticuffs. Another couple we know had a blazing, frying-pan-throwing row over the date of Saddam Hussein's invasion of Kuwait. Somehow, though, I don't think casual tops or the unsuccessful assault on a small oil-producing country was the actual issue.

As one gets older, one tends to mellow. When I was in my twenties I used to think, Don't get mad, get psychotic, but by the time I was well into my forties, I discovered that living well is definitely the sweetest revenge.

Glutton for punishment

We're not one of these families who can leave ornamental bowls of confectionary lying round the house. We don't have a wine rack because the essential ingredient for a wine rack is wine, so we drink our wine as we buy it. Doesn't everyone? Our house is an alcohol-free zone, except when we are drinking.

My life has been plagued with addictions. I gave up smoking long before I was legally allowed to start. Then I took it up again. Now I have only a very occasional cigarette to remind myself why I gave it up in the first place.

I drink to forget why I drink in the first place and eating is not so much a survival skill but a recreational hobby.

Over the years I've come to the sad conclusion that a Whopper and Diet Coke do not cancel each other out, that broken biscuits have more calories that whole ones and that if no one (that is, your mother) sees you eat it, yes, it still counts.

Skinny people annoy me. There are rules and reasons for skinniness and the first is that skinnies sometimes forget to eat. The reason skinnies don't eat is because they don't have time, so they say. My husband falls into this category.

How long does it take to scarf down a cheese and salad roll? Three minutes max? It's a bit like saying I didn't have time to breathe, or blink or sweat.

I used to be a closet eater. No, I didn't eat closets, I just used to hide in them with a bag of custard cream buns.

Eating is the most important meal of the day. I am, therefore I eat. Live to Eat. Let's have none of this Eat to Live rubbish. Life is what happens in between rounds of roast pork, watercress and wholegrain bread with mustard sandwiches.

Fruit and vegetables are overrated. There's as much nutritional value in a Cherry Ripe as there is in a bag of cherries. You just have to eat more Cherry Ripes in order to extract the goodness.

There's nothing like buying fresh green vegetables for dinner and boiling them in a pot. When they turn grey you know it's time to serve them up for the family dinner.

Cordial now has 5 per cent real fruit juice. I'm not sure what the other 95 per cent is but I'm sure it's irrelevant in God's Great Plan.

When deciding on a restaurant – All You Can Eat is really the only choice. Don't forget to wear your biggest pair of elastic-waistbanded slacks when you go. We have to look good as well as eat tip-top quality food.

Don't feel bad about being overweight. It's not your fault. It's that heinous, apathetic mother of yours who not only bottle-fed you – shock horror – but she also forced tinned baby food down your throat as well, and at an innocent age where you couldn't voice your protest. That sort of behaviour borders on child abuse.

Everyone knows that real mothers only ever breastfeed and that, in the freezer, they have trays and trays of different coloured pureed vegetables that they cooked up themselves.

The ultimate betrayal, aside from your mother's sloth, is when someone you know gives up smoking and drinking – and starts to spleen-vent on about the benefits of clean air and a sober mind. Crikey, the way they bang on.

The most difficult part is sitting around waiting for them to come to their senses, which you know, of course, will eventually happen. No one could possibly stand to feel that bracingly self-righteous for any length of time. I think I'd rapidly shrivel up and die without all those additives and preservatives to keep me alive.

Chocolate is full of endorphins. Why spend an hour at the gym when you can get the same high from eating a bar of Cadbury Dairy Milk watching the Men's Singles Finals at Wimbledon?

I could take the dog for a walk, but I'm scared I might get run over by a bus or abducted by aliens. The safest bet for maximum enjoyment of life is to bunk down in my lounge room next to the fridge with my finger poised on speed-dial for the local pizza, liquor and cigarette delivery services.

Sometimes life can only be understood and appreciated

backwards. If I have one deep regret, it's that I didn't track down and sideswipe that car with the bumper sticker saying 'No Fat Chicks in Polyester Leggings'.

Loud and proud

Pride comes before a fall. Just ask anyone who's bought a pair of strappy stilettos and had to pop pain-killers in order to move and mingle at a party, and then, while teeter-tottering off to the nearest bar, fallen from a great height and severely bruised her ego. It gives the term 'fashion victim' a whole new meaning. But I'd rather die a diva than a dag any day.

Before I reached the age of forty, it was perfectly acceptable for me to lie on the bed with a coat hanger hooked into the zip of my size 12 black cords and slowly inch them closed over my size 16 hips. Suffering excruciating abdominal cramps was a small price to pay for the spray-on look.

These were the very same cords I split down the bum when attempting a triple spin on a pair of rollerblades trying to impress a group of unimpressionable fifteen-year-old boys.

On the day I wore my gorgeous new bathing suit to the local Wet and Wild, two things stood out and neither of them was the brand new waterslide. As soon as I plunged head-first at breakneck speed down the vertical face of the slide, with the G-forces crushing my cheekbones to a pulp, I knew I'd made a tactical error.

After what seemed like an eternity of sliding, I whiplashed to a halt, knowing full well that what was left of my pride and dignity was now tightly wound around my ankles, in full view of several teenage boys – again. I'm not sure, but they might well have been the same ones I had mooned at the rollerskating rink the previous day.

When I finally decided to lose some weight, it was during the reign of Queen Jane Fonda, who stretch lycra'd me and most of my generation into semi-permanent lactic acidosis. It was now official: pain was the definitive black.

With my tendons and ligaments threatening to ricochet up to the roof of my rectum, I told myself that even if my legs did drop off, at least the rest of me would be in perfect, enviable shape. But by that stage I could have convinced myself that a mammogram or an anal probe would be a barrel of laughs, just as long as I looked absolutely fabulous while it was happening.

These days it takes more money than pride to be fashionable. I recall an ego trip to the shops when I found the most perfect little black dress; it came with the most perfectly obscene price tag. I've always had an uncomfortable feeling that I only bought it so I could tell people how much I thought I was worth.

She who dies in the most expensive little black dress still dies.

Black is good if you have put on a few grams recently. Black is even better if you've put on a few kilos recently. The only time black is not good is if you suffer from dandruff or flaky scalp; then it's always best to go *Miami Vice*.

Against my better judgement, I had my fortieth birthday and slowly it began to dawn on me that the secret to life was a comfortable pair of tracky dacks, a windcheater, a pair of ugg boots and leaving fashion statements to my daughter.

Clothes don't maketh the person, the person maketh the person. It's what's under the clothes that matters. Therapy has taught me that grace and dignity are far more important than labels. Unless, that is, the label reads: 'Reduced – 20% off'.

Fashion fades —style is eternal.

Leaving pride behind when dealing with difficult family members is a bit like wearing rayon or polyester. It gets easier as one gets older. Let your mother win some of the age-old family arguments for once. If your pride is wounded and you can't get over it, then at least pretend to.

Grace and dignity will eventually prevail over wounded self and instead of wishing your worst enemy be struck by random lightning, wish her all the very best instead. And mean it.

But next time there's a thunderstorm — secretly stick a lightning rod on her chimney top. Not that I'm advocating revenge, just basking in the warm afterglow of my judicial sense of extreme pride and prejudice.

Until sloth do us part

Sloth is my middle name. Sloth is also a very old and very dear friend of mine. Sloth is finding it difficult to get out of bed in the mornings, even if the house is on fire. I'm of the belief that if I haven't had a shower or opened the curtains then the day hasn't really begun.

I seem to operate in a different dimension to the rest of society: gravity sucks me into a downward spiral and I have no choice but to indulge in my natural state of semi-hibernation, regardless of the season.

Sloth lies somewhere between my two huge, recumbent sleepy cats curled up next to my television-watching teenage daughter who is urging me to go to the shops for some more icecream.

Sloth is the not-so-fine layer of dust that gets frantically feather-dustered just as my mother pulls up in the driveway. It's also the washing that I sometimes conveniently forget three days running before finally sticking it in the dryer, regardless of the temperature outside.

Sloth is watching eight hours of television and passing it off as extensive and dedicated research into the entertainment industry. It takes a lot of strength and willpower to stay glued to the television for that length of time.

I don't, horror of horrors, recycle anything. I don't do dishes unless the sink is brimful with dishes and debris. The bedroom floor doubles as my wardrobe. When I run out of toilet paper I use tissues rather than go to the shops. Sheets and pillowcases can sometimes last as long as two months and I never got to church on Sunday because I desperately need that sleep-in. It's hard work doing nothing all day.

Sloth is pretty much a victimless crime, unless you have a husband or children. If you do, it's then your duty to get off your bottom at least once a day to microwave them a creative dinner.

Watching all the red-faced, early-morning joggers as I hide in my garden smoking a cigarette just brings out the couch potato in me. Instead of feeling guilty I just go back to the couch, snuggle deeper under the rug and channel surf lifestyle programs.

I plan on getting an immunisation before the gym bug hits me again. Doing nothing costs, well, nothing. Nothing ventured, nothing gained – or spent –my money stays in the bank.

It's not so much that I'm sitting and staring out the window as it is that I'm contemplating the rich fullness of my inner spiritual life.

Sloth is the art of looking busy while doing absolutely nothing, something I managed to excel at just before I resigned from my job at a call centre. I was so burnt out that I started cutting off callers in mid sentence.

First I cut off annoyingly verbose callers. Then I cut off anyone with a foreign accent I could not understand. Eventually, I decided to hang up on every third caller. That was about the time I handed in my notice and renewed my anti-depressant prescription.

I could think of many more examples, but I just can't be bothered.

Greed, is it good?

According to Gordon Gekko, the leading character in the 1980s movie *Wall Street*, greed is good. 'Greed, for lack of a better word,' says Gekko, 'is good. Greed is right. Greed works. Greed clarifies, cuts through and captures the essence of the evolutionary spirit.'

I'm guilty of being greedy in the eighties. We were building a house and I wanted it all, wanted everything and I wanted it right now. Having it yesterday was not soon enough. I wanted to get the house finished as soon as possible because my real goal was to have children, as many as possible, because I thought the more children I had the happier I would be. I was desperately greedy for lots of children. Less isn't more. More is more.

Later on I learnt that greed was not so good when it came to having children because I was overwhelmed by the responsibility. Not that I don't love the ones I've got but it's impossible to be my natural greedy and selfish self when there are three little people depending on me.

I feel like the mother bird who is constantly on the hunt for insects to feed her voraciously hungry baby birds, all with their beaks permanently open to receive the food she brings them. The relentless squawking gets on my nerves and grinds me down. Only it's not insects my kids are after, it's playstations, rollerblades, clothes, overseas holidays, lunch money and more, much more.

I have had to sublimate my own greed under the sheer weight and force of my children's needs. I don't come first in my life any more. My kids might beg to differ. I bought a bar of chocolate to share and my son decided he would be the one to divvy it up because when I did the divvying I always gave myself more than everyone else. A power struggle ensued. He thought I was being very greedy. I told him that, as the unselfish mother that I am, I was just watching out for his waistline.

It should come as no surprise, then, that my kids have inherited the greed gene. After opening their Christmas or birthday presents comes the incredulous 'Is that it?' look on their faces, a bit like the one I used to have myself as a present-opening child.

A good indicator of whether you are greedy is to ask yourself this: if you won Lotto just how much would you give to charity? Or, would you give in to the temptation if someone, though not necessarily Robert Redford, offered to pay you $1 million to have his wicked way with you for one night? Would innate greed overcome morality? It's a question I've struggled with for many a pointless year.

Every so often, when I'm sitting in a comfortable armchair, greedily tucking into a bar of chocolate, I dream about that great, greedy Lotto win, the one that would mean never having to do housework or paid employment again. Yeah, right. Me and the rest of Australia. Of course, it would help if I got out of my armchair and spent my hard earned cash on a Lotto ticket rather than confectionary.

9

Q: HOW WELL CAN YOU COOK THINGS UP?

A: The Four Fs – Fatness, Fitness, Food and Fashion

The faked chef

When I first saw Jamie Oliver and heard about his program, *The Naked Chef*, I thought I was going to be watching a pornographic cooking program with a drop-dead gorgeous Englishman whipping up some cream in the kitchen.

Just occasionally, when I have the whole house to myself and am in the mood, I put on some classical music, strap on a frilly apron and get out the extra virgin olive oil and the Jamie Oliver cookbook.

The stove is not the only thing that gets turned on in my kitchen on those afternoons. Jamie Oliver is the only man on this earth who can make baked ricotta cheese look and taste sexy. Even his lisp has a seductive quality about it.

So how can you tell if olive oil is extra virgin? Only Popeye could really answer that question. It's not the 'virgin' bit that puzzles me, it's the 'extra' bit. Maybe that's why he's called Popeye.

Everyone's eyes popped out of their head the other night when I cooked Black Bean Asian Delights – from a packet, mind you, to all intents and purposes it's still recipe cooking by my standards, especially as we have been living on anything that can be defrosted and microwaved in recent weeks.

I was very excited, so excited that I also chopped up some real onion and garlic before tossing the lot into a sizzling wok full of virginal olive oil. So virginal it was still blushing. I would have preferred to rub some extra virgin olive oil into Jamie Oliver's chest and slide around the kitchen floor with him shouting 'Pukka! Pukka!'

As would my husband with Nigella Lawson, the only woman I know who can make a sumptuous banquet out of a frozen pig's ear.

Although Jamie and Nigella are very easy on the eye, it's the two fat ladies, with their propensity to cook everything in fat, who I used to love dearly, especially their recipe for which you have to find some very, very lean duck, or turkey or chicken with absolutely no fat on it at all, and then proceed to dress it with love and tenderness in streaky bacon.

Theirs was good old-fashioned wholesome cooking in a time before the nutrition nazis politically corrected not only the airwaves, but also the supermarket, the kitchen and my children's ears.

Although my kids like their salad rolls for school lunches, on the weekends the whole family gets ready for a different fare: bacon and eggs and a sit-down in front of the television for the weekly *Simpsons* marathon, which keeps us enthralled for at least five hours.

If we put tomato sauce and a bit of parsley on top of the bacon and eggs you can just about get away with saying it's a healthy dish.

She died with a frying pan in her hand

Easily, the room that creates the most arguments in our household would be the kitchen, where the biggest zone of contention lies somewhere between the frying pan and the decaying contents of our frost-free fridge, our very own awe-inspiringly low standard of living. Not quite good enough for my mother's white glove, but nor is it quite bad enough for a Health Department overhaul.

Like most families, we lie somewhere between that heaven and hell called Real Life.

When it comes to cooking, we are discerningly deep but sometimes we can surprise ourselves by being superficially shallow. Our motto? The family that fries together, stays together. Through thick and thin.

When it comes to our frying pan, a quick wipe-out with a paper towel is only ever justifiable when the smoke detector goes off. We prefer to recycle our fat, building up layer upon layer of goodness and nutrition in which to coat our humble cuisine.

In other words – want not, waste not, something my mother taught me when it came to runny eggs and Brussels sprouts.

We learnt how to fry our food properly when we had overseas relatives stay. All food in the north of England, which includes Scotland, is deeply fried in a particularly profound and meaningful way. I believe that deep-fried confectionery now replaces haggis as Scotland's favourite national food.

According to these relatives, we weren't putting enough fat in the frying pan. The bottom had to be covered by at least

3 centimetres of hot, bubbling oil before we dropped our bread in, they said. Golden brown and fried to perfection, the bread was then wrapped around a piece of streaky bacon so that, when you took a bite, fat dripped down your chin. *That* was frying food properly

As of yet, no one's ever been disobedient enough to wash the family frying pan. Aside from such cleansing being sacrilege, we try to deter revolutionary behaviour as much as possible in our household.

Aside from a sheep's stomach and its contents, the other thing I just can't swallow is ancient, leftover, fridge food. Leave something to stew in its own juices for long enough and Charles Darwin's Theory of Evolution will eventually transpire. Your expensive, out-of-season strawberries, unlike your overpriced children, will develop a fur coat and a functioning brain before abseiling down the fridge and heading out the front door for good.

Other miscellaneous items in there, wrapped in foil, are, like Pandora's box, best binned intact than let loose on the general public.

I don't want to be remembered for being responsible for the new and improved Bubonic plague in the twenty-first century. I'll just leave that one to the health and hygiene experts who invented bulk food bins for supermarkets.

However, the biggest threat to the survival of children-kind is their intransigent, militant extremist belief that the litter bin lurks behind the lounge suite. Lolly wrappers, Vegemite sandwich crusts and forgotten homework abound. I can detect white trash quicker than the Iraqi Army can sniff out arrogant, money-hungry American businessmen.

But there comes a time when even the pigs have to clean up their own pigsty and that happens every Psycho Saturday.

Once a week I like to see all the rooms clean at exactly the same time.

Like most girls, my sister and I learnt our housekeeping skills from our mother who instilled in us over the years that if you shout and scream loud enough housework will eventually happen. If it doesn't get done over the next twenty-four hours Psycho Saturday simply morphs into Scarier Sunday.

So by Manic Monday, everyone is ecstatic to go back to school and work which leaves me basking in the Eternal Sunshine of the Spotless House.

Unless of course it's the school holidays where everyday is an exercise in the futility of fundamental change and cajoling the kids to open the games room curtains before noon is tantamount to a full day's hard work.

Tomorrow never diets

The other day I received an extremely rude letter from my doctor telling me to go on a diet, start exercising and give up smoking and drinking – and to 'adopt a healthy lifestyle management plan'. I was not amused.

Aside from the occasional heart attack I'm in very good health and the thought of giving up smoking makes me want to reach out for one immediately. As for the 'E' word, I can assure you I'm talking about ecstasy.

There is no intoxicating rapture involved in exercise. I could no more jog around the block than I could fly to the moon without the aid of mind-altering substances. No pain, no gain? No pain, no pain as far as I'm concerned.

Does running away from your problems count as exercise? I went on a liquid diet once but even chardonnay and beer palled after three weeks. I'll do anything to lose weight – except give up my favourite foods. Or start exercising. People who gallop for 5 kilometres every morning are the same people who fight you for a parking spot closest to the shops so they don't have to walk as far.

I once tried a pre-breakfast jog taking our very surprised dog with me, but I decided it's no good trying to keep up with the Joneses. I'll just have to drag them down to my level instead. I did learn one important rule of thumb though. Never, ever jog past Baker's Delight on an empty stomach.

I ate some baked beans for breakfast once and thought they were off until I read the label and found out they were preservative – and salt – free.

For lunch, I tried to sex up a slice of Ryvita by topping it with salad but it still felt like a dry peck on the cheek instead of hot, sweaty fornication with Robbie Williams.

When my kids are safely in school, I'll indulge in my ongoing, intense, passionate love affair with Mr Cadbury right in front of the television and drink a glass of good wine to my good health, not that there's any such thing as a bad glass of wine. If love makes the world go around, alcohol makes it go around twice as fast. But don't worry, I'm OK. I'm not as think as you drunk.

Fashion is whatever fits

I'll let you in on a little fashion secret that clothes designers appear to have not stumbled across. One size does not fit all.

Not unless you are a standard size 10. One size fits, well, one size, and one size only.

One-size fashion has never fitted me: I am at least three different sizes on any given day, depending on what time of day it is. Everyone knows they weigh less in the morning, so generally the best time of day to buy clothes is before six am.

Shopping for clothes at night, especially after eating a huge curry, is fraught with danger, and we're not just talking here about fitting into a pair of jeans.

Fitting rooms indeed. Why they call them fitting rooms I'll never know. Not only is there usually not enough space to swing a caterpillar, but none of the clothes ever fit anyway. They should be called fatting rooms. And who do they think they're fooling with those skinny mirrors?

I'll tell you why they are called fitting rooms: because every so often a fat, angry woman chucks a fit in one of them. I heard a story about a woman who, on a 42°C day, tried on a one size fits all top that was at least two sizes too small and it got stuck. There was no way she could leave without ripping it off. She ended up leaving with only a red face and never shopped there again. In fact I think she avoided the entire shopping centre for at least a year.

For a long time fashion was, for me, whatever fitted. If it fitted, I bought it. This is back in the early 1980s when there was no such thing as fat etiquette for the figure-challenged and the biggest sizes could only be found in garish colours.

My teenage daughter is a constant size 10. For years I honestly thought that I spent many a happy hour buying her gorgeous clothes. Sadly, it took me many years and many, many dollars to realise that anything her mother liked and bought for her was automatically given the kiss of death. Looking back on it, I was her worst nightmare, at the very least in the clothing department.

While she would be in the fitting room successfully trying on the latest fashions, I would be outside alternating between screaming at the hapless salesgirls to turn the music down and having a hissy fit trying to persuade my daughter to open the locked fitting-room door so I could see what my hard-earned money was being spent on.

Instead of our shopping together being a bonding experience, it was all rather a disaster that served only to remind me that the past does indeed repeat itself. My mother used to do the same thing with me. Must be a genetic thing.

In the nature versus nurture debate, one size does fit all, especially when it comes to designer genes.

Handbag therapy

When women are depressed they go shopping. When men are depressed they invade another country looking for weapons of mass delusion in the shape of their paternal figure. Let's not beat about the Bush here.

Shopping with a handbag big enough to hold all the documents of your history is normal for most women. Retail therapy might be great but you won't find your mother's approval at Myer, not unless you have a handbag the size of a world leader's ego.

Thinking you'll find the right handbag, like finding the right man, is an exercise in self-delusion, which is why most women have at least fifteen handbags. We put more effort into finding the right handbag than we do into finding the right man.

Your handbag, like your marriage, will change over the years. But most important of all, your handbag and your husband both have to be big enough to accommodate all your previous baggage. Size does matter. The handbag has to fit comfortably over your arm, be colourful enough to maintain your interest and neutral enough to go with the rest of your life.

When we got married my first handbag was a snappy little black leather number with a gold clasp. It matched our relationship. Now I carry a suitcase just to go get milk and bread from the shops. Men carry keys and a wallet and, if they are vain, a comb.

Back in the 1980s retailers tried to introduce handbags for men. I could have told them it wouldn't work for suburban husbands. My husband would rather chop off his arm than carry a handbag over it in public. When I ask him to hold my handbag for even a split second he acts as if its writhing with poisonous snakes, not a receptacle for money, keys, hairbrushes, lipsticks, bills and receipts, used tissues, tweezers, little white mice in plastic containers, nail polish remover and decade-old letters from overseas relatives.

Why do men feel their sexuality is in question if they carry their wife's handbag for thirty steps? Do we question our sexuality when we walk out of Bunnings carrying a bag filled with hammers and nails?

I've taught my thirteen-year-old daughter that a handbag, like a man, is a necessary evil. She now has one the size of a matchbox, a handbag that is, not a man, just enough to carry her own personal emotional baggage in.

My husband carries his keys and comb in his back pocket; my two boys have nothing but fluff and lint in theirs. Their mother lugs around a suitcase the size of a psychiatric hospital, but she's hoping to go down a size or two some day.

10

Q: who PEELS at YOUR house?

A: Therapeutically Speaking

Beauty and the unbequeathed

There are more instruments of torture in my bathroom cabinet than were ever used during the Spanish Inquisition. Those eighteenth century wusses had no idea how to inflict pain and suffering. We new millennium women have rectified that – we know how to suffer sufficiently.

Take a pair of tweezers, for instance. It's the smallest, most innocuous looking devices that usually mangle and maim the most. Plucking my eyebrows into thin, submissive lines always left me feeling and looking like I'd just been stung by a thousand angry wasps. So I gave up on that and took the easy way out: I applied hot wax instead.

If you ever want to know what an application of hot wax feels like, stick your hand into an active volcano for thirty seconds. Scrape what's left of your skin off with a wire brush and you will have a vague idea of why women are always in a bad mood.

Unless you are a short, stocky bouncer at a nightclub, the hair on your head should never be removed. I pay good money for some young thing who wasn't even born when I attended my first rock concert, to inflict excruciating agony on my bonce.

Remember the old streaking cap? Back in the 1980s I wimped out with general anaesthetic every time I needed my hair streaked. Thank goodness for twenty-first century foils. I suffer foils gladly now. With any luck the streaking cap, along with false eyelashes, G-strings, platform shoes and orange lipstick, will be permanently housed in the annals of history.

I own at least seven different hairbrushes: long ones, wide ones, thick ones, thin ones, round ones. Plugged into my bathroom sockets are curling tongs, crimping tongs, straightening tongs and three different styles of hairdryer, yet I still can't get my hair to look like I've just walked out of a salon. My husband keeps it simple: he has a comb in his back pocket.

Is it just me, or does anyone else check out their profile, pat down or boof up their hair and smear on some lippy all in one swift motion as they pass a mirrored window? The passing glimpse as disturbing as *Funniest Home Videos*, rather like glancing back over your shoulder at Sodom and Gomorrah and turning into a pillar of embarrassment.

How many people on the other side of that mirror have rolled on the floor, hysterical, watching men adjust themselves, women hoik up their bras or had the delight of witnessing a pimple squeeze?

I can't help but check myself out in every other window, although I draw the line at gouging out my facial blemishes with my long, expensive, polished, acrylic nails. Checking out is based on the same principle as coming across a car accident: there might be devastation and carnage but you just can't tear your eyes away. If I happen to have my children with me when

I pass by a mirror it's also a good idea to check to see I haven't suddenly grown two horns and a forked tail.

I've even been known to check out my reflection in a puddle on the ground, although, to be quite frank, it's not my best angle.

OK, so I'm a vain old woman who wants to be Peta Pan.

If you want to witness a scene from Dante's *Inferno* just get up close and personal with your well-lit bathroom mirror. Meandering rivers of red fire – formerly known as a peaches and cream complexion – interrupted only by a huge bulbous beast formerly known as your nose. Those black spots on your huge bulbous beast will go forth and multiply into colourful spots fighting for room on your face, just as you are opening your telegram from Queen Camilla in the year 2045.

Never wonder again why most adult social functions are held under dim lighting.

Life is full of bitter frustrations and calamities, but you do eventually find the right hairdresser. I'm sure the kids don't mind living only on Cornflakes just so I can tell a lot of white lies about the grey of my hair. In fact, not only should they not mind, they should just be eternally grateful I gave birth to them in the first place.

Is there something wrong with wanting to look like Elle McPherson's younger sister when I'm eighty-seven?

I know, I know – beauty is in the eye of the beholder – Yada, yada, yada. It's what's inside that matters – etc., etc., etc. Beauty is only skin-deep – Blah, blah, blah. But who cares about having a lovely liver or a gorgeous gall-bladder? It's just as well the mirror reveals only the outer layer of my personality disorder.

At a party I went to recently, I was appalled to discover that all I wanted was for someone to turn down the volume control.

If the music had been that of a 1970s glam rock band, then I couldn't have had the volume loud enough. That's a dead giveaway for my age. Intolerance is not skin-deep; it penetrates right to the inner core of my nervous system and brings out the grumpy old woman in me.

It would appear that I am ageing against my will.

I don't mind getting old so much as I hate getting wrinkles and liver spots. It's just as well wrinkles don't hurt or I'd be in immense pain. Liver spots should stay on my liver. Now, just as I finally feel I'm getting my head together, my knees are starting to fall apart.

By the time I've exfoliated and deforested, waxed and waned, pillaged and plundered, shaved and plucked, foiled and blow-dried, cut and shaped, pinched and squeezed myself down a couple of decades, I'm simply too frayed and frazzled to even contemplate leaving the house.

Peeling back the layers of family therapy

Today's society not only encourages, but expects women to have a postgraduate career, a loving partner, happy, motivated children, an even greater postnatal career, followed by a well-deserved nervous breakdown. If you're not highly strung and stressed out to the max, you're simply not trying hard enough.

No wonder family therapy is necessary to help us nut out those vitally important issues in life, such as whose job it is to peel the vegies for dinner.

No one wants to peel them, but everyone expects a healthy, delicious, creative surprise at six o'clock.

Household job rosters appear to be the universal solution. But job rosters, like family self-help manuals written by single people, have good intentions, but bugger all practical application in the real world.

In *Little House on the Prairie*, Ma and Pa Ingalls never had any problem getting Mary and Laura to rise at the crack of midnight, milk the cows, collect the eggs and mend the fences.

The Brady Bunch never had a jobs-around-the-house problem either, that being less to do with an effective roster system and more to do with good old Alice, the housekeeper.

It's unlikely that the earth would stop turning if my kids voluntarily rose off the couch and offered to help prepare dinner, but it would certainly rock my world.

Many parents have spent hours creating complicated, colour-coordinated children's job roster spreadsheets dating well into the next millennium. Never confuse activity with productivity. Multicoloured spreadsheets, like your lazy offspring, do not peel the spuds and carrots for dinner or wash the dishes after it.

A computer-generated lifestyle might fool Nanna and Granddad into thinking your household is an efficient, well-oiled machine, but its purpose is purely aesthetic. If our family were a business, we'd have declared bankruptcy before we started. We are less efficient at running our household than Basil Fawlty is at running a hotel.

It's not easy nurturing and maintaining a constant state of dysfunction. A lot of hard work is required. Pulling together as a team requires softer voices and effective communication.

Radical, unworkable thought processes such as these could put family therapy out of business quicker than you could say 'That's the way we all became the Brady Bunch!'

But the earth, like my head, is still spinning in the Universe, my children's bedrooms remain toxic waste dumps and the second generation of vegetables is now on the market. Pre-peeled, pre-cut, pre-packaged pre-frozen pieces of household harmony, more expensive than the fresh alternative, but considerably cheaper than family therapy.

Off yer trolley

Ever wandered around the supermarket aisles looking at what other people are buying? It would be interesting to have my weekly groceries analysed. A psychologist would definitely think I was off my shopping trolley.

It takes a very brave woman to walk around Woolies with her Tim-Tams on display.

When I was overweight my trolley was full of Diet Coke, diet yoghurt, low-fat this and no-fat that. When I was skinny it was full of crisps, Coke, full-cream yoghurt, fatty fried foods and high–fat this and extremely high-fat that.

In the years BC (Before Children) my trolley was full of lean cuisine, little packets of very expensive cat food, fluffy little mouse-shaped toys and 20 kilo bags of kitty litter. No wonder pet therapists are in vogue.

Ten years ago my trolley was a shrine to my inner obsessive–compulsive control freak. Overflowing with Ajax, Glen 20, Mr Muscle and microfibre dusting and polishing cloths, I was truly a Domestos goddess. A spotlessly clean house was the only option – just in case the Queen popped in for tea. Or my mother.

My postnatally depressed and anally retentive self filled my trolley full of chocolate covered somethings and everythings.

Even the laxatives were of the chocolate variety. When my kids were little they thought it was normal to have chocolate sauce poured over their broccoli and peas. When I told everyone that my children ate up all their vegetables, it was never a lie.

During my masochistic stage, I made sure my pre school children were bored and hungry so I could I hype them up on lollies and red cordial for that added zing of excitement as I screamed around the aisles.

Once in the supermarket, it didn't take long before my schizophrenic multiple personality kicked in and I needed two trolleys, one for each personality. It was only a matter of time, then, before my paranoid–schizoid phase just meant that I shopped at the local garage at midnight so no one could see what I was buying.

It was when I got to the supermarket checkout and mysteriously found my trolley full of beer, wine and spirits that I knew it was time to see a therapist.

I got sick of spending $300 on groceries and listening to every member of my household whingeing there was nothing to eat in the house. Shop until you drop? No way! Don't shop. I stopped shopping, gave the kids lunch orders every day and had pizza delivered every other night of the week.

Chocolate – the new chardonnay?

I was raised in the belief that 'totallydisasterousmarriage' was all one word. I also used to think that monogamy consisted of having one husband too many.

Then my children grew into teenagers – against my specific orders, I might add – and my husband and I finally became united against the common enemy.

Before the arrival of children, our sex life was hotter than Mark Latham's diaries. Now, with three boofy teenagers taking up all the available couch space in the house, sex has become as furtive as sneaking a quick smoke behind the garden shed when you've told the rest of the household that you've given up.

The best substitute for sex is chocolate. If you can't farm your kids out so you can indulge in a dirty weekend, sublimate your libido by scoffing down a Mars Bar. John Travolta, I once heard, can eat three Mars Bars at a sitting. What! Only three? What's *wrong* with the man?

Well, is chocolate the new chardonnay?

As I discovered recently, sucking on a bar of chocolate is not only as soothing as sucking on a bottle of chards, but it's also just a little bit more socially acceptable during school assemblies.

Chocolate gives you the same endorphin rush as sex without your kids having to sleep with the radio on. When my oldest son came home from school this week with yet more fundraising chocolates to sell, my endorphins shot up to red alert.

We never actually sell any to family, friends or neighbours; it just gets left in the middle of the lounge room until the box is empty.

Sometimes my need for a sugar rush is greater than my need for oxygen. I've tried stashing my Toblerone around the house, but the kids can sniff out Swedish chocolate quicker than *Today Tonight* or *A Current Affair* can ferret out a dysfunctional family.

Rewarding my children with chocolate and sending them out to play cricket is a bit like making them eat fruit in front of the television: I call it a healthy compromise. Other people might call it crap parenting.

Of course, sending them out to play cricket with an apple or banana would make far better sense. But since when did far better sense have anything to do with the way I raise my children?

So, is chocolate better than sex?

I guess that all depends on who you're sharing your chocolate with.

The truth about cats' and dogs' names

If you look back on your life from childhood, patterns of behaviour emerge that tell you the existential truth about your goals and your aims in life, how your parents brought you up and who you really are.

I believe that, when it comes to naming our cats and dogs, fragments of our tortured childhoods emerge from the foggy wilderness of our split-off memories.

Our first cat was called Whiskey. Our second cat was called Brandy. My sister's two cats are Shiraz and Chablis. Our current dog is called Tipsy and our latest cat is black and named Cofi.

It doesn't take a Sigmund Freud to work out the existential truth about my family history. Yep, you guessed it. We are a family of animal lovers.

One of my earliest childhood memories is of dressing up my first cat, Whiskey, in doll's clothes, tucking her up tightly under the blankets and holding her down. Whiskey would hiss and spit back at me while I sang her sweet lullabies. From that time on I knew I was destined for maternal bliss.

Around about the time I gave birth to my third child, my beloved sister purchased a pair of very neurotic cats from the Cat Haven. She was under the erroneous impression that having two cats was the same as having three children. I put her on the straight and narrow about that particular misconception.

When my husband and I were DINKS (double income, no kids) we had a cat called Boris; I tortured myself every time my precious little pussikins escaped from the house. If Boris looked as if he were about to scratch himself he was rushed to the vet. When we became SITCOMS (single income, three children, oppressive mortgage), Boris was given short shrift when he tried to vie for our attention. Every time he scratched himself, it really annoyed me.

When Boris finally went to Kit-e-Kat heaven we decided to get a pair of kittens. From then on, sleeping through the night was only ever in our dreams. The kittens slept all day and ran amok all night, crying and meowing.

But that wasn't the worst part. The worst part was that I finally had to admit to my sister that perhaps she was right after all.

Brainwashed

Ever feel like you are involved in a sinister cult with a leader who is continually trying to brainwash you? Chances are you haven't joined the Rajneeshes or the Moonies – you are simply living with your mother.

Not only are mothers travel agents for guilt trips, flying you to hell and back in the rear seat of their broomsticks, but they are also dry-cleaning agents for your brain, with the ability to scrub free any nasty little independent thought processes you may have the audacity to possess.

A house is not a democracy, it is a ship. With Mother well and truly at the helm, it is a dictator ship.

My brain has not only been washed, but it has also been on spin cycle for several years. Only when the spinning finally stopped did I realise it was me suffering from vertigo and not the rest of the world. In the outer suburbs no one can hear you scream.

It was only when all three children were at school and I had six selfish spin-free hours to fill each day that my brain recovered from postnatal concussion.

I pre-soak my neurons every other night with a good splashing of Southern Comfort fabric conditioner on the rocks. But washing the grey matter in your family is not about separating the colours from the whites. If your mother washes your brain, it's your father who hangs it out to dry and it becomes your therapist's job to gently iron out the creases.

It's part of my daily cleansing routine to gently exfoliate the blebs and bumps of my children's medulla oblongata into realising that life does not owe them a living.

There are places to eat other than McDonald's, Bey Blades are not the answer to playground popularity and allowing a thirteen-year-old to have an unlimited credit card is, generally, not a viable option, not unless you want to be taken to the cleaners.

More importantly, I'm going to brainwash my children into thinking they can actually have a point of view in our house without me marching them off to the laundry – as long as their point of view fits into my plans.

So when Mum rings up to talk to me, I tell her I'll have to ring her back because I am far too busy doing the washing.

My family is definitely a cult above the rest.

Mothers' attention deficit disorder

When I read the Parliamentary Inquiry into Attention Deficit Disorder I decided that it was not only my problem, but it was also my diagnosis.

In other words, I was not just garden-variety stark-raving bonkers, I was completely and utterly mad MADD, that is, I was suffering from Mother's Attention Deficit Disorder.

Just ask my children. A couple of years ago when I was extremely busy and they would come to me with their multitude of problems and concerns, I tried desperately not to make eye contact with them and fobbed them off as quickly as possible so I could get back to watching other people's problem children on currents affairs shows.

It would take a monumental effort from their MADD mother to give them the correct amount of time and focused attention they needed so they wouldn't grow up to be serial killers – or even worse – a politician or a defence lawyer.

So when I got a phone call from the deputy principal telling me that one of my children had nicked a $50 note out of my purse and was waving it around the school canteen, I replied that it was all my fault as I hadn't been paying my children any attention lately.

The fact that I was working sixty hours a week as well as

attending to my own personal lifestyle simply didn't cut the mustard in the right side of my brain.

My kid was clearly shouting from the rooftops, '*Hello, Mother!* I'm going completely MADD here.' It was a sobering moment for me and at that stage in my life there wasn't a lot of those.

It was either give up excessive drinking or give up excessive working. Or cut down considerably on both unless I wanted to see my children playing a starring role as some other mother's problem on the current affairs shows.

There's a faint hope for the former and I managed to downsize the latter, but at least I know I'll never again see my kids wave a $50 note under the deputy principal's nose because these days, after cutting down my working hours, I simply can't afford to have one in my purse.

Perfection vs Good enough

I feel as though I'm trying to live in a world of perfection and I'm just not good enough, not as a mother, as a wife or as a cleaner of our castle. I can never get the house clean enough. The grotty state of the shower sends me *Psycho*.

My cleaning never feels good enough unless every nook and cranny shines to perfection. If they don't, I feel as though the walls are starting to crumble around me and destruction and devastation are descending like a dark cloud. Either that, or my mother is coming to lunch.

Perfection exists only in my head and in other people's lives, especially people in television shows and movies. Shouting at my children to get them to help tidy up the house is not so much an exercise in cleanliness as an exercise in futility. Still, I manage to do it on a regular basis anyway. It gives me a sense of control over my destiny, even if it doesn't get the dishes done or the lounge room tidied up.

In a perfect world I'd win a million dollars and hire a cleaner for the rest of my life.

I just can't help myself when it comes to consummate achievement for ultimate fulfilment. Forget about a peaceful and harmonious enough world; I seem to be programmed with the desire to eliminate all dirt and dust off this planet.

When I couldn't achieve that lofty status – world cleaner-upper – I was seduced by the dark side of the force to find myself warm enough and comfortable enough in a messy, untidy house but with the nagging feeling that maybe it wasn't quite right enough, but it didn't feel quite wrong enough either. It just felt bad enough. And that was good enough for me.

So at the end of the evening, with the dishes still piled up in the sink, I sit down with my family in front of yet another *Simpsons* marathon, a box of chocolates in one hand and a glass of wine in the other.

That's what I call a shining example of a perfect world.

Don t worry, be happy

Happiness is a state of mind. Happiness doesn't live in the future, it lives with me at this very moment. I can make up my mind to be as happy or as unhappy as I want to be.

Serenity is looking at your galvanized, secondhand, prominently-situated shed and thinking – it isn't so much bore-stained as character-coloured. It's all a matter of perspective.

When I look into our carport and see lawnmower engines, tyres, steering wheels and other miscellaneous items retrieved from the recent bulk rubbish collection, I don't see a pile of useless junk cluttering up my parking space. What I see is my husband and middle son engaged in a bonding process collecting the parts necessary to make a motorised go-kart.

Which is a spinaround from the obsessive–compulsive control freak who suffered insomnia if the skirting boards hadn't had their daily polish.

I don't apologise for the state of my house anymore, I just celebrate my new state of mind.

I have to see my midlife crisis, depression and rapidly approaching menopause as potential for emotional growth. Either that or an extreme makeover with expensive Botox injections and liposuction will ease me through my twilight years.

Even the therapy profession has individually suffered some sort of depressive traumatic crisis and survived intact, which is how they became therapists in the first place.

Before I understood that, I thought they just sat in their ivory towers dispensing wisdom for a living. Learning different made me realise that the world isn't made up of black and white, it's a blurry, murky shade of grey.

As Cher sang in 'If I Could Turn Back Time' while wearing that infamous gownless evening strap – if I could turn back time, I would hope to learn earlier on in life that self-reflection, yoga and meditation are the best drugs in the world.

There's a place in your mind that no travel agent has a brochure for. It's cheaper than an overseas holiday or admission to a private psychiatric hospital, and you can float off to it anytime you want and still function in the real world at the same time.

The world's best-kept secret is that there is more entertainment inside your head than there is on Foxtel or than mind-altering substances could ever provide.

So turn off the television and turn on to life. Meditation rules. After all, hundreds of Buddhist monks can't be all wrong.

Now all I need is for my husband and son to move their bonding process into our character-coloured shed and I would be one very happy born-again mother.

Zen and the art of motherhood

The other morning I woke up, leapt out of bed filled with joy at such a beautiful day. Had a shower, shampooed, conditioned, exfoliated, scrubbed, brushed, towelled and invigorated my mental health status back down to defcon 5. Made the bed, opened the window and smelled the coffee. I love the smell of decaf skinny cappuccino in the morning.

Went outside to the garden and self-reflected and meditated myself into a blissful Zen state. Watered my plants and marvelled at the sheer beauty of being alive. Decided to plant a rose garden next to the shed and walked back inside to find my three children starting their new day with a serious bout of sibling rivalry and my best carving knife.

'Don't bleed on the carpets, I've just had them cleaned,' I screamed, still maintaining my tree-hugging outlook on life.

'There's no food in the house,' they whinged, meaning that all the Coco Pops and Fruit Loops were gone. 'Eat bread,' I snarled, while meditatively adopting a complicated yoga pose. 'But it's brown and there's lumps in it.'

As far as my children are concerned, only white bread is kosher, so, to all intents and purposes, there was no bread in the house. I gave them instant mashed potato for breakfast instead. As I calmly poised myself into an even more strenuous mind-calming yoga position I kept one eye on the window, just in case welfare showed up to arrest me for not providing my kids with a meal that had the four food groups healthily represented.

It's only a matter of time before that happens. I believe legislation is about to pass that will permit hidden cameras to be forcibly installed in your kitchen for the nutrition police to keep a healthy eye on you. When that happens I will be conducting my self-reflection, meditation and yoga from the comfort of a nice padded cell.

Breakfast over, it was time to drive the kids and their scaly mates 400 metres to the local school. I pulled into the carpark, dumped the kids, pulled out and nearly sideswiped an oncoming car whose driver had the audacity to beep the horn angrily at me.

I then expended more energy refraining from flipping the bird than if I'd actually done so. I was in the wrong, but that was beside the point. Zen and Buddha had done a bunk on me: I had worked myself up to defcon 1.

Got home and got even more bent out of shape because the kitchen, spotless upon waking, now looked like a bunch of marauding baboons had fought a territorial battle in it, which is closer to the truth than not.

Deciding that I needed some cool refreshing air, I stepped out into the garden again, took some deep breaths, absorbed the early morning sunshine and lit up a cigarette. Then decided I was not a morning person after all – and went straight back to bed.

Mum's the word

Adult daughters need their mothers. In fact, some adult daughters can't seem to live without their mothers.

Mothers have broad shoulders and warm hearts. My own mother has nothing better to do than sit at home all day waiting for my daily crisis call in which I get to dump my day onto her.

My mother doesn't have any issues in her own life; even if she did, mine are far more important than hers.

I'm under the impression I've had a dreadfully hard life – and I tell her so. On a regular basis. She listens with care and empathy and tells me she understands what I'm going through. But I get a vague, uneasy feeling she's thinks I'm self-indulgent, high-maintenance, personally intrusive and disrespectful of her time and ability to cope with my incessant petulant demands.

She might be very fond of me, but my behaviour is clearly driving her insane.

I have another vague and uneasy feeling that what would give her great satisfaction is to pick me up by the scruff of my neck and deposit me in the long grass for some timely self-reflection while she closes her ears to my howls of dismay.

It might be her way of telling me to take a bit more

responsibility for my life, starting with cutting the umbilical cord and learning how to breathe on my own.

It's not like I'm dependent on her or anything. Just because I suffered separation anxiety and panic attacks because, when I was 42, she took an overseas holiday without me doesn't mean I can't push my own mood swing.

The scary part is, I think it's me she needed to take a break from. Now there's a sobering thought. Quick, pass the chardonnay, please. And put a teat on it while you're there.

Apparently, I've been taking my mother for granted for too long now. But a small gift should do the trick. Just a small one, mind you. The more expensive the gift, the bigger the guilt.

I don't have to let her know just how guilty I feel about using and abusing her – a bag of marshmallows will do, just to show her how warm and soft she really is.

Of course, what I'm actually doing is giving her a piece of myself so that when she sits down to watch Patsy and Edina abuse Saffron and dunks a marshmallow in her hot chocolate she will remember me with sentimental warmth and affection instead of frustrated grief and irritation.

The therapeutic benefits of chocolate-coated marshmallows can never be underestimated.

I've finally learnt that there are worse things in this life than turning out just like your mother.

The thinking client's therapist

The best part about therapy is that, unlike your husband, even after ten years your relationship with your therapist will still be in the honeymoon stage.

Therapy isn't the real world. It's a fantasyland where you, the client, are the centre of someone's undivided attention. But however seductive that is, it's a means to an end, not an end within itself.

Fantasyland is also where fantasies happen; all of a sudden you find yourself wanting to be your therapist's best friend. This sort of attachment is beneficial as long as it never occurs.

In fact, for a long time I thought my therapist was only one-dimensional and didn't ever leave her office. In the evenings she just filed herself away and appeared like magic the next morning, bright, ready and alert.

You don't need to know that your therapist probably wanders around Woolies wearing a daggy Fleetwood Mac T-shirt, arguing with her overweight, chain-smoking husband and obnoxiously behaved children.

My therapist, wearing a cool pin-striped power suit, was assigned to me during a hospital stay for postnatal depression with my third child, now ten.

Seeing as I used to rank psychologists slightly below used car salesmen, politicians and journalists on an integrity scale, I didn't hold out much hope.

The first psych I ever saw asked me if I was breast or bottle fed and the second told me there were people far worse off than me. The third psych went psycho on me and I couldn't get out of there fast enough.

But my fourth psych seemed to be made of sterner stuff. She was nice enough, but it used to annoy me that all she ever wanted to talk about was my mother.

It wasn't until she told me a very lame fart joke that, in my eyes, she gained any street credibility. Up until that point I thought she was a bit of an Ice Queen, possibly based upon the fact that she was so competent at her job.

Most of my friends had therapists and we'd go out for lunch and compare and contrast. I was always smug because I knew that I had the best therapist. What I didn't know was that I had a very transparent case of what the psychology world calls transference. This means transferring a past relationship, usually, but not always, your relationship with your parents, and projecting your positive (or negative) feelings about them onto a current relationship, usually with your therapist, who becomes the good (or bad) parent. So your therapist, in effect, is role-playing your fantasy parental figure for the sake of the therapy. No matter how badly behaved you are, your therapist will still approve of you. The whole idea is to work out your childhood issues to your satisfaction.

Over time transference will fade and you realise that, increment by increment, therapy has actually worked and you can now hold your own in the real world.

Just as there is no such thing as the perfect parent, there is no such person as the perfect therapist, just the good enough one. Your mentoring therapist gets a big kick out of seeing you get better, in much the same way a good enough parent can sit back at their child's high school graduation and think, 'I didn't do such a bad job after all.'

The good, the bad and the ugly

Trying to stay positive, optimistic and generally uphold a bright outlook during life's ups and downs, as well as having to continually bolster the rest of your family's flagging self-esteem – especially when you just want go off to crash and burn somewhere private – is emotionally exhausting and physically draining.

Teaching self-responsibility to aggressive little children is not only time-consuming, but, fundamentally, it is also self-defeating.

I get sick and tired of taking responsibility for my own actions and there are moments when I just want to lay the blame at someone else's door. If my mother's at home, that's always a good place to start. But when the door was slammed in my face, that's when therapy seemed like a good idea.

Who wouldn't enjoy spending the best part of an hour whingeing and blaming everyone but themselves for the poor state of their life, knowing you can come back next time and do it all again and the therapist isn't going to throw you out?

But just because your therapist validates your dysfunctionality in a soft cooing voice doesn't mean that, like your mother, she can't see your faults either.

Here's some good, some bad and some pretty ugly stuff I've learnt on the path to realising that my glass of semillon sauvignon blanc is actually half-full and not half-empty, contrary to what I previously thought.

The Good is when you see a therapist.
The Bad is when you fall in love with your therapist.
The Ugly is when your therapist falls in love with you.

The Good is when you realise it's all about your mother.
The Bad is when you think your therapist is your mother.
The Ugly is when you want to crawl into your therapist's lap
and stay there forever.

The Good is when you can see your mother's point of view.
The Bad is when your mother can see only her own point
  of view.
The Ugly is when your therapist can see your mother's point
  of view.

The Good is when you finally get angry with your therapist.
The Bad is when your therapist finally gets angry with you.
The Ugly is when you introduce a set of darts into the
  therapy session.

The Good is when you want to slap your therapist's face
  because she reminds you of your mother.
The Bad is when your therapist wants to slap you in the face
  because you remind her of her daughter.
The Ugly is when you realise you both have sadomasochistic
  tendencies and slap therapy becomes a mutually
  enjoyable pastime.

The Good is when your mother finally sees a therapist.
The Bad is when your mother chooses to see your therapist.
The Ugly is when your mother and your therapist decide to go
  on holiday together.

The yellow brick road of therapy isn't easy. It is best seen as a
journey rather than a specific destination. But with your mother
as a back seat driver, do expect to hit a few speed bumps and
potholes along the way.

11

Q: Shouldn't children look after their Parents more?

A: Secret Girls' Stuff

Save the children

The United Nations Save the Children Fund is a very worthwhile organisation. But what about chipping in to a Save the Parents Fund instead? Or, better still, donating some well-earned dosh to my preferred charity, the Save the Long-Suffering Mothers Fund, where money is raised for put-upon parents to wickedly indulge ourselves away from our greedy, selfish and demanding children?

If my kids were less egocentric, they would pool their pocket money and send me off to the Bahamas for a guilt-free holiday, with a couple of airport bonk-buster books for good measure.

I love books, especially the big, heavy ones on psychology. They come in very handy when my children are misbehaving and need a good whack on the backside.

Not that I smack my children. Well, not in public anyway.

Someone from the Save the Children Fund knocked on our door recently. I said, 'Thank goodness! My children are so expensive. Just make the cheque out to cash, please.' I was most disappointed when they asked me to cough up some money.

I desperately need more funds to save my children from boredom in the school holidays. Surely a significant sign of bad mothering is a bored child.

Children are supposed to have a rich imagination, but these days, if a child shows the slightest sign of anything imaginative, we send them back to school at the end of the holidays for urgent reprogramming.

My job as a mother is sometimes saving my children from their own inventiveness and fantasy, to say nothing of my wrath as a mother when I realise that several cans of expensive deodorant have been pilfered from my bathroom for their personal usage.

I had no idea such ripping and enthralling entertainment could be found in a bottle of atomised spray until I realised the ingredient that doubled the fun was fire. Their flair for flamethrowing far surpassed last semester's school reports. I was almost proud of them.

Am I the neglectful mother of naughty, destructive children? Or am I selflessly giving them enough space to allow maximum development of their rich imaginations without constant parental supervision? It sounds good, doesn't it?

When I discovered vegetables were missing from the fridge I was pleased. My kids are eating wholesome nutritious food at last. Or so I thought, until I realised they were pelting them down the street at the other kids in our neighbourhood.

Next holidays, instead of becoming a cash-strapped, burnt-out basket case, I'll just give them a bottle of Impulse, a couple of tomatoes and a box of matches and kick them out of the house – for their own good, of course.

I'm sorry

If I could live my life over with the knowledge and wisdom I've accumulated over the years I reckon I'd still get it completely wrong again.

There's something disturbing happening in my world. It's the unwitting ability to repeat the traumas of my past without actually realising it at the time.

Nowadays I apologise for everything.

Even my computer has the capacity to apologise. When there's no email to download I get a message, 'Sorry – You have no email.' My teenage daughter translates this to mean, 'Loser – You have no friends.'

I apologise when my children come and tell me that I've ruined their lives because I won't update their mobile brick to the latest model. I explained to them that a mobile phone is a means to an end not an end in itself but would some chocolate icecream help recover their lost status and self-esteem.

Chocolates are an apology. So is a bunch of flowers. Every woman knows it and every man would be wise to remember it.

When I hit a motorcyclist with my car two decades ago, I visited him in hospital with a huge bunch of flowers and said, 'I'm sorry!' His very expensive and esteemed lawyer took that as a complete admission of my stupidity, incompetence, worthlessness and guilt and tore strips off me in court. My apology cost me $300 and my driver's licence for twelve months.

Given the same circumstances, I would offer the same apology for exactly the same reason I always apologise to my children when they accuse me of being stupid, incompetent, worthless and guilty, which usually occurs on a regular basis.

Taking on board the guilt of your children and the guilt of global and minor catastrophes is part of the burden of being a mother.

Sorry is the hardest word to say and love does sometimes mean having to say it.

Bridgetting the gap

I'm confused. In fact I'm very confused. I'm confused as to why Bridget Jones – who has the perfect life – wants to get married and have babies?

What is *wrong* with the girl?

She has a fantastic job. Sorry, not job – career. Working mothers have jobs. Singletons have careers.

Our Bridgey has a career in publishing. As well as an enormous flat in the centre of London with lots of caring, nurturing friends popping in all the time.

Even at her heaviest Bridget is still skinnier than I could ever aspire to be, and my knickers are half the size of hers. Anyone who thinks that their life is a complete and utter disaster because they weigh 52 kilos – needs a psychiatrist, not another diet.

And, she has the Divine Hugh Grant and Mr Sensitive Colin Firth snotting it out in the gutter for her.

Here's a few excerpts from Bad Mother's diary.

Subtitled (Married With Three Children. The Edge of Insanity.)

Number of pooey nappies changed since wedding night and producing two little Darcys – 22 896.

Number of times I've wished I could sing 'All By Myself' and actually be all by myself: Never happened. Nothing more than wishful thinking.

Number of times I wished I was still single, living in London – with Hugh Grant's shoes lurking under my bed: Don't even go there.

Number of times my kids have nicked lunch money out of my purse before chucking their cheese and Vegemite sandwiches into the bushes on the way to school: Too numerous to mention.

Number of times the school has rung me to let me know of behaviour transgressions: I believe they finally ended up putting us on speed dial.

Amount of unnecessary guilt I've suffered during my life: Enough to keep a therapist occupied for at least a session a week for the last ten years.

The number of times I've wanted to strangle my argumentative little sods, *aka* children: At least three times per day per child.

The number of times I've kissed and hugged my kids simply because I gave birth to them: At least three times per day per child.

Number of times I wished I'd never had children: Not once. Not ever. Not once have I ever wished I'd never given birth to them.

Maybe I don't envy Bridget Jones as much as I thought I did because as far as I'm concerned, there's only one thing worse than having children. And that's not having them.

Fender bending

When it comes to driving cars in a reckless fashion, I'm living in the Danger Zone. I just can't help myself. I have to push the boundaries to see how far I can bend them before they break.

Only the other day, decked in my pyjamas and with the petrol tank sitting under empty, I drove the kids to school. Unless I'm living on the edge, I'm just taking up too much room.

Most of my fender benders happen in shopping centres where parked cars and signposts jump out and hit me. 'It wasn't my fault, officer, it jumped out and hit the back of my car.'

I've yet to learn the delicate intricacies of parallel parking. Reversing into a car spot seems wrong, so I go in head first, doing a wheel re-alignment as I mount and dismount the kerb, leaving passersby wondering how on earth I managed to get my driver's licence in the first place.

Driving down the freeway applying my lippy, smoking a cigarette and talking on the mobile phone at the same time – as I do –isn't bad driving, it's honing my talent for multiskilling.

It's not easy being an atrocious driver. It's taken me many years to get this many careless habits.

A couple of decades ago, I lost my driver's licence for a year. Not my fault, of course; it was the motorcyclist who ran a green light who was in the wrong. As a result of losing my licence for twelve months my husband got to be the designated driver and I got to be the designated drinker.

My husband assures me that teenage boys are full of testosterone. They drive fast cars and can drink beer till it's coming out their ears – but they're never drunk. In fact, everything they do is done over the limit in order to prove their manhood. My daughter's mechanically inclined boyfriend assures me that riding in cars with boys is not about getting from A to Z safely, it's getting from A to Z sideways in a huge cloud of grey smoke.

While we women sometimes like to think we know what's under the bonnet of a car, playing the helpless role is much more fun.

I had a flat battery at the local shops, but luckily I also had a pair of jump leads. A woman stopped to help and we were doing fine and dandy until this utterly gorgeous Brad Pitt lookalike in short, tight shorts offered to help. We both went to pieces and pretended there wasn't a brain cell between us.

As we feasted on eye-candy, Brad managed to fiddle around under my bonnet and very soon had my motor purring like a kitten.

I needed to sit down and have a cigarette after that.

Five reasons why mother has a pounding headache

1 Wet towels don't get dry under the bed

Unless you want to grow a tropical rainforest under the bed, hang your towel on the drying rack. Reafforestation is a very noble thought, but let's first try to keep the bathroom tidy before we reclaim the rest of the world.

Wet towels get left on the bedroom floor because, as we all know, mothers have way too much spare time on their hands. The fact that it takes just as much time to hang up the fluffy bath sheets as it does to avoid the sodden, stinky lumps on the carpet is irrelevant. It's the act of rebellion that counts. A bit like men who conveniently forget to put the toilet seat down.

While it's maddening that my kids drop putrid-smelling towels on the floor at random, it's downright disturbing that one of my sons not only hangs up his own wet towels, but that he also puts his dead and dying socks in the laundry basket for me to resuscitate. The other two scatter theirs around the house, treasure-hunt style, leaving me to collect the ones that even the dog found too disgusting to chew on and bury.

2 The sharpest rollerblades in my kitchen

The relentless rustling and swishing of children rollerblading in my house constantly grates on my brain, rather like the way my thighs rub together on a hot and sweaty day. Appealing to a child's sense of respect for law and order has about as much chance of actualisation as trying to get my two cats to quit scratching the couch by persuading them that I can't afford to get it recovered.

3 How many wet towels does it take to change a light globe?

Avoiding wet towels while rollerblading in the dark is rather difficult. No one in our house, including my electrician husband, feels it is in their job description to change a blown light globe. We'd all rather sit in the dark, sulking and glaring daggers, than be the loser any day.

Even when we've blown every other bulb in the house, I have to prise my husband out of his armchair to go out and buy some more. When he wants to know why only he can do it, I tell him that I'll buy the light globes if he writes the tender loving blurb on my mother's birthday card. Like most men, he'd rather buzz-saw his right hand off than whisper sweet nothings into his mother-in-law's ear.

Half an hour after this discussion there is light at the end of the lounge room. Unfortunately, it turned out to be an express train heading straight towards us.

4 Alarming smoke alarms

You can't rush important jobs, you know. After eighteen years, three children and two burnt carpets, we finally got around to installing the smoke alarms we bought nearly two decades ago. Three hours later, when the burnt Sunday roast set them off, we disinstalled them.

During that window of opportunity, one of my progeny, who shall remain nameless and blameless due to the lack of compelling evidence, had a cigarette lighter blow up all by itself in his bedroom, which melted a hotplate-size black hole in his bedroom carpet. Last time that happened was when my husband, having finished his shirts, left the hot iron on the carpet and walked away.

Smoke detectors are fantastic when you have pyromaniac children, but leave a lot to be desired when you are a serial toast burner.

5 Where's the Panadol?

Painkillers disappear faster in our house than fine wine at a fiftieth birthday party. Either I drink more alcohol than I should or there's a black hole in the back of our bathroom cabinet that's suffering more than me.

The noise level in our house drives me to drink. The kids turn up the television to drown out my nagging and even the goldfish are starting to sound louder than usual. That's when I need a painkiller and a good lie down.

It's not that I'm a Bad Mother, I just don't care for the job sometimes.

With friends like these, who needs an enema?

Your best friend is the one who holds back your hair as you heave into the toilet bowl after an exceptionally great night out in Northbridge. Then again, I've had so-called bosom buddies who have not only not held my hair aloft, but have grabbed me by the back of the neck and pushed me face down into the toilet and flushed.

Sometimes, when we don't know ourselves very well, we're attracted to people who want to hurt us.

My sister is one of my best friends. I'm not completely sure whether our friendship was born out of a need to combat the common enemy – our parents – or whether we just clicked, and now rattle along like a steam train on a country jaunt.

Either way, the best part about sisterhood is that I can afford to be myself, which is fantastic because I have neither the money nor the means to be anybody else.

Those truly bonded in personal tragedy – in other words, women who have children of a similar age – don't need daily, weekly or even monthly correspondence. Sometimes whole years can go past and when you do get together you simply take up where you left off.

I have a friend like that, a rose without the prickly thorns. Our friendship goes back to our childhood when we used to run around the streets clad only in our navy-blue knickers, amusing ourselves putting rocks on a railway line, setting the local bush on fire, rollerskating down a stormwater drain, making caterpillar jam or just catching tadpoles and watching them turn into handsome frogs. I just can't help but hear schmaltzy violin music playing in the background when I reminisce about those golden olden days.

A true friend will revel in your madness, forgive you for falling asleep in your fettuccine after one too many glasses of red wine at lunch and listen quietly and endlessly as you cry on her shoulder about some of the less than savoury people in your life.

A not-so-true friend will hold you solely responsible for the vagaries of the British Rail system when connecting journeys are nearly missed. If you haven't learnt your lesson by then, you certainly will when you realise that anyone who spreads malicious, poisonous gossip about other people, is also stabbing you in the back on a regular basis.

Thankfully, friendships like that come and go quickly. It takes an extraordinarily large amount of low self-esteem and confidence to covet companions who take personal pleasure in abusing you.

Sometimes one grows out of a friendship. While painful, the only thing you can do is to face the fact that your address book needs to be culled every year or so.

It's absolute wretchedness to realise that losing one friend can result in losing a whole group of friends — until you realise that perhaps you weren't on such good terms after all. After a while, you come to the sober understanding of just what a narrow escape you've had.

I haven't always displayed wisdom in my choice of friendships. Sometimes I've been the drab moth overshadowed by the glitteringly colourful social butterflies who would much prefer I had simply stayed in my cocoon.

Moths, when only viewed under the cover of darkness, appear drab and insignificant, but once out in the sunshine they can dazzle with their glowing iridescence. When that happens, it really gets up the proboscis of the alpha butterfly.

A long time ago, I was worried that I didn't have the socially acceptable number of friends in my inner circle. Now I can count my true friendships on one hand and casual acquaintances on the rest of my fingers and toes.

I've learnt the hard way that you can't shake hands with a clenched fist.

Shredded nerves for breakfast

If you thought the Cold War was over – think again. It rages on relentlessly behind closed doors at least three times a day. Two Superpowers vying for supremacy in the same household.

Not the USA and the Soviet Union this time, but you and your obstinate, obstreperous offspring. The mother of all battles is fought at the dinner table. It would appear that he who dies with the coldest vegetables on his plate wins.

What is it about uneaten broccoli and cabbage that brings out the sergeant-major in mothers? Children have amazing stamina. What started out as a pleasant family dinner has now turned into a masochistic feat of endurance.

Even the promise of a never-ending box of Tim-Tams is unlikely to lure them into submission. Once the rules of engagement have been laid down, it's a clear case of may the best toddler win.

Take heart, though, in the fact that a toddler has never willingly starved to death. They may not eat their minced beef, but at least there are plenty of slugs and slaters – the other white meat – in the back garden to crunch on.

The evening meal is not so much an exercise in morosely picking at your fish with your fingers, but a veritable minefield of non-conformity and subordination. I know, because my mother used to serve me up a healthy dose of gourmet guilt as a main course every evening.

Those supper-time skirmishes have nothing whatsoever to do with what's actually on the plate in front of you, so much as being a cauliflower combat zone where the War of Independence is either won or lost.

I spend a lot of time fighting for peace in our household, but I've lost the Battle of the Bulge hands down because, like so many other mothers, I have a tendency to eat all the leftover food from the table rather than waste it.

Food fights have nothing to do with food. There's nothing civil about war, whatever it's fought with, and fighting for peace is like promoting sexual intercourse for virgins.

My family's Cold War hots up considerably when the dishwasher needs loading; that's about the time most people go missing in action.

I prefer to think of my family as functionally dysfunctional rather than as a casserole of catastrophic grief. Some of us prefer to bask in the rainbow of illusion rather than discover that the pot of gold at the end of it is just another dish to wash.

As the emotional baggage handler in our household, I'm at risk of dislocating both shoulders because I sweat the small stuff all day, every day.

I'd rather be responsible for feeding the starving millions than conduct a daily royal commission into who spat their toothpaste onto the back of the bathroom door.

Life's not fair. It's either immoral, illegal or just plain fattening and recognising these facts is a very liberating experience.

Stupid parents

Teenagers, are you sick and tired of your stupid parents harassing you about the state of your bedroom? Fed up with your sad, nosy parents annoying you by asking if you had a nice day at school? Feel you know all the answers to life without ever having bothered to ask any questions?

If you do, then you are a typical teenager.

There is no book on earth to prepare parents for the advent of teenagers. There's many a sugar-coated book, sure, but they simply do not cover what happens in your household. The things that you are too scared to speak about in case no one else has experienced it.

There is even less information available to prepare parents for the transformation of their beautiful, compliant child into a sullen, rebellious, alienated, monosyllabic, grunting teenager. 'It won't happen to my teenager,' you say, but, like Christmas, it creeps up on you, slowly and insidiously.

Late at night, while my teenage daughter lies sound asleep in her bedroom, I am wide awake wracked with guilt that, despite my best intentions, I am not bringing her up properly. It's easier to pick the winning lottery numbers than it is to second-guess my teenage daughter.

She enjoys swanning around the local shopping centre with her friends on a Thursday night. You know, one of the crowds of teenagers who keep the economy ticking over nicely. She yearns for a Mr Burns lifestyle on a Homer Simpson budget.

Nothing can prepare an obsessively houseproud mother for the mess teenagers make. Cereal bowls left festering under the bed, piles of smouldering clothes and wet towels left in the doorway. She is immaculate in her personal hygiene and dress, but her excuses for the mess are limper than a Melbourne Cup hat the day after the big race.

When I was a teenager my room used to get untidy, but not the catastrophic state my daughter's gets into. Things are moving under her bed. There is life under there, but not life as we know it.

Sometimes I feel like a hostage rather than a parent. 'Trapped' is the word. I feel trapped. In fact, the older she gets, the more worn out and trapped I feel. The more I worry. Then I worry because I'm worrying too much.

My one and only consolation is that one day when she's older and, of course, a lot wiser, she'll have teenagers of her own and realise parenthood equals sacrifice.

Revenge is definitely a dish best served cold.

Zen and the art of menstrual cycle maintenance

One day while buying tampons, it suddenly occurred to me that there would come a time when I would no longer have need to spend exorbitant amounts of money on non-taxable items such as feminine hygiene products.

That made me very sad. I was upset to think that one day I would not menstruate. This thought also gave me the heebie-jeebies because it would mean I was also approaching menopause: in other words I would be getting old and, like most middle-aged people, I just don't do old.

But by the time I'd had a hysterectomy at the age of forty I realised I had been duped by Mother Nature all along. Not having my periods meant I could wear white trousers all month round.

My first period arrived on my doorstep when I was twelve. By the third day I was sick and tired of bleeding profusely and always having to be aware of leakage. The novelty had worn off and I felt boggy and bloated. I also suffered horrendously from cramps and diarrhoea.

Bleached surfboards with belts were the only style available back then, the only notion of wings being that of an integral part of an aircraft, not yet something that held your pad in place.

After a few months I came to realise that the only civilised way of dealing with periods was tampons.

Back in the 1970s, many mothers believed that tampons were not only unhygienic, but they were also somehow associated with the loss of their daughter's virginity and were dead against their use.

A friend of mine's mother believed in the old wives' tale that you must not bathe during your period. My friend was not allowed to shower, have a bath or wash her hair during this time. Logic didn't come into the argument. Of course, as we all know, this is the time we need to shower more often, not less.

Men have always been rather afraid of menstruating women, associating them at this time with the unclean. But as I said, logic has nothing to do with women's working parts. Even my normally broad-minded husband gets thingy about women's reproductive organs.

Never send a man out to do a woman's job. Once, long after I'd given birth to our three children, my husband bought me tampons and, although I admire him for doing so, did he have to come back with the cardboard applicator ones?

When you think about it, a period is the loss of a potential pregnancy, the loss of a life never born, not just a messy, annoying week in any given month.

It wasn't until I was trying for a baby that I realised what having a period was all about. It was something to rejoice in. It was something that was going to turn into a placenta and nourish my babies. I looked upon menstruation differently after that.

I now suffer my periods through my daughter. Life still goes on. And on. And on. When my two boys ask me why my daughter is allowed to have a day off school every month, I tell them the truth. They reckon it's not fair. So I explain to them that life isn't fair because if it was, men would have periods and give birth and women would drink beer and watch football.

Give men-a-pause

If my husband can fly a plane all the way to Avalon, Victoria, and spot the runway from 3000 metres, why does he have so much difficulty finding the sugar in the pantry?

Men need extreme guidance around the house. Even with the lights blazing they are still in the dark when it comes to learning what makes us tick like a time bomb.

They might be able to hunt down and kill woolly mammoths, bench-press a ten-seat dining table, kill tarantulas with their bare chests and drink beer in the sun for days on end, but if you so much as hint at a slap of sunscreen or suggest getting a seeing-eye dog, they accuse you of questioning their masculinity.

Why would a man want to rip up several square metres of perfectly adequate brick paving just because there's a slight dip in it that is invisible to the naked eye, only evident in a heavy rain?

This isn't just my bloke. My neighbour confirmed the same phenomenon in her husband. Finding the milk bottle that cleverly concealed itself behind the carton of beer is beyond them, while they display ultrasonic powers in exposing otherwise undetectable dips in their brick-paved ego.

The pergola might be propped up by life-sized noxious weeds and the internal walls bear more scars and patches than Kostya Tszyu because it would appear men have this debilitating case of tunnel vision that enables their eyes to pass over those parts of their lives that simply doesn't interest them.

Such as grocery shopping. A little secret all wives know is never let your other half do the food shopping. They may be able to perform brain surgery, build fifty-storey skyscrapers or fly the space shuttle to the moon and back, but ask them to tootle off to the shops and purchase some fruit and veg and they'll come back with stuff that even a starving Ethiopian would reject, just so they can get home quickly to nurture and cherish their four-wheel-drive. They'll spend many happy hours fiddling under the bonnet or polishing away non-existent scratches, but when you go off your face at them for buying spotted fruit, it suddenly dawns on them they missed a spot on their four wheel drive and slowly back out the front door.

When I notice a blown light globe, rather than replacing it, I get bent out of shape remembering every single job my husband needs to do. I might've been looking forward to seeing him when he gets home, but instead, by the end of the day, I'll scream blue murder for a job he didn't finish fifteen years ago. What's most disturbing about this is that I can see the logic in my own argument.

When, in the 1980s, we built our house, it was the law of diminishing returns that dictated most of the work gets done in the first two years. After that, you'd be lucky to get your bloke to find his own clean socks in the morning.

When we first got together, my husband would come clothes shopping with me. Not just tag along, but actually try to help me find the perfect outfit. The mix and match outfit he offered was a polka dot top with a stripey skirt. I think he might have had less blood in his brain at the time though because, as he admitted years later, it was the thought of well deserved sex at the end of the shopping spree that fortified him. Even Sensitive New Age men will do sensitive New Age stuff when they get horny enough.

I went on holiday to Brisbane last year and, while I was there, got a phone call from my husband asking where our son's Cub Scout shirt was. It was well hidden on top of the second drawer of his dressing table. I subsequently suffered a panic attack.

It doesn't seem fair that men don't suffer panic attacks because of an unfound shirt or a broken fingernail before a social function, or that they don't writhe in agony because they were the only parent to forget to bake a cake for the classroom stall. Men don't grieve over their child's last baby tooth. Ever known a man to wake up in the middle of the night worrying because it started raining and there's washing on the line?

He complained to me that I'd changed over the years and got sulky when I laughed. Of course I've changed. I'd be horrified if I was the same person I was twenty years ago. Aside from the obvious ageing, he hasn't changed much at all.

When I get into bed at the end of the day, there's just one more job left to do. Let the cat out the door.

Flowers and chocolates might get him gasps of appreciation, doing the dishes and sweeping the floor give him a better chance of having his wicked way with me. But I'll take the flowers and chocolates anyway.

Just imagine what the world would be like if it were women only. No wars, no crime, no remote control fights. Just lots of fat happy women sitting back drinking wine.

Why women are grumpy

Why is it that even after a good night's sleep I can grouch out of bed and start hollering hysterically at my children because there's milk and sugar spilled over the benchtop? It doesn't take a lot of practice to rocket from zero to menopause within 2.3 seconds when I've been woken from a dream where Hugh Grant is gently nibbling on my toes by the sound of carnage in the kitchen.

I no longer feel the need to constantly seek my parents' approval for everything I do and I no longer have a fear of confronting disgustingly disagreeable and invidious strangers in public venues.

Why? Because I'm getting old and grumpy, that's why.

Several years ago, while on holiday with family and friends, we came across a man and, presumably, his daughter as we were walking along a jetty. The man was teaching her that it was OK to stamp down hard on a puffed-up blowfish.

I puffed myself up to twice my normal size and, to everyone's horror, verbally stamped on and deflated this Philistine, this savage of monstrous proportions.

Upon telling my like-minded mother, she not only approved of my behaviour, but she was also very proud of me.

It's not the first time I have stood my ground against vexatious little bags of hot air.

On a plane trip from Queensland to Perth, a toddler terrorist persisted in kicking the stuffing out of the back of my seat during takeoff. In my most ingratiating voice and with a sickly smile on my face I politely requested the father to please ask his offspring to immediately resist and desist booting me up the bum.

The father puffed himself up like a pompous parrot and informed me that his son had every right to do whatever the hell he liked and if that included punching me up the date with his Weeboks, then so be it.

I had just spent two weeks trawling the theme parks with three hyperactive and argumentative children. I also had the worst case of tinea on record and now this pumped-up pinhead not only expected me to take it up the rear end during takeoff, but to be grateful for the privilege as well.

I don't think so. Batten down the hatches, people, we are expecting some severe turbulence right about now.

I raised my voice for the benefit of the passengers hiding behind their broadsheet newspapers, and told him that when the seatbelt sign went off, I was going to move to the spare seat directly behind him and enjoy bouncing his scrawny arse all the way to Perth.

Had my husband and kids been there (for some inexplicable reason Qantas put me at the front and them at the back of the plane) they would have preferred I risked lower-bowel perforation from an impacted gym shoe than cause an interstate incident.

The hairs on my chin bristle at the thought of such injustice gone unpunished. Sometimes I think I was put on this earth simply to extract retribution from some of the more perverse and pig-headed members of the public.

I've screamed across acres of parkland at boys tormenting a duck with a stick. I've wound down the car window to bellow some of the finest and most exquisite expletives imaginable (some not even found in the *Oxford English Dictionary*) at errant motorists, before ending the repartee with a very enthusiastic bird-flip.

It's not just other people who cause me to flip my wig, I can do that all by myself, thank you very much.

When I take the dog for a nice, relaxing walk and the wind lifts my newly-washed hair horizontally and vertically at the same time, I feel myself wanting to jump up and down, to stamp my feet, having an overwhelming urge to kick something. At this point the dog looks at me very warily.

Maybe I'm just not getting enough sex or I'm eating the wrong kind of vitamins or something, but I seem to be wearing my nerves on my sleeve, and the rest of the world in general, and my family in particular, seem to take great delight in rubbing in the salt.

Perhaps the real reason we bang on about breaches of promises in our lives could be because, as we get older, we slowly but surely regress into an infant state of mind.

This is where basic tolerance and understanding of life's little foibles is, once again, way beyond our comprehension. We become our own centre of attention for whatever is left of the rest of our life.

Then our children get to pick out our nursing home and we can settle down with the knowledge that when they visit us twice a year, all our service and sacrifice for them has been more than worthwhile.

12

Q: Why DIDN'T Someone Teach Me THIS at School?

A: What I have learnt in life

What I have learnt in life

- ☑ That I want to come back in my next life as one of my cats.
- ☑ That life is not black and white, it's a murky shade of ambivalence.
- ☑ That it is OK to give up breastfeeding once your nipples have fallen off.
- ☑ That paying an exorbitant fee to join a gym doesn't make you fit. You have to actually go and work out to get some benefit.
- ☑ That I'm not flexible enough to put my foot in my mouth, but I manage to do it on a regular basis anyway.
- ☑ Never binge on garlic olives if you have an important function on that night.
- ☑ After ten years of therapy, I've learnt that therapists not only have mothers, but they also have mother issues.
- ☑ That as the older child, my sister adored me, but that I was too busy tormenting and teasing her to notice.
- ☑ That there's no such thing as a normal child.

- ☑ That the time a teenager needs love the most is when they deserve it the least.
- ☑ That it's now compulsory to use the men's loo if the queue at the women's is a mile long.
- ☑ That it's better to regret not saying anything than it is to regret saying it in the first place.
- ☑ That while Batman will live on forever, Superman was just as vulnerable as the rest of us.
- ☑ I've learnt that a brisk walk in the woods is a good substitute for Prozac.
- ☑ I've learnt that public pool water doesn't turn red if you have a pee in it.
- ☑ Good fences make good neighbours.
- ☑ That your walls can be covered in Vegemite fingerprints even if you haven't had Vegemite in your house for years.
- ☑ That the lawn always grows quicker when the lawnmower man is on holiday.
- ☑ That it's a waste of time buying a non-remote-controlled garage door.
- ☑ That just because my children are doing my head in doesn't mean I don't sometimes yearn to be pregnant again.
- ☑ Never to email anyone after a glass of wine or four, not unless you enjoy apologising profusely the next morning.
- ☑ When played by two brothers, Monopoly and chess can be bloodsports.
- ☑ If you want to see a good movie, read the book.
- ☑ That cleaning your house in the school holidays is like drying yourself with a towel while still under the shower.
- ☑ That, with seventy-five channels on cable television, there's always an episode of *The Brady Bunch* annoying someone somewhere.

- ☑ That biology doesn't make you a mother. Being a mother makes you a mother.
- ☑ Even therapists get irritable with their clients.
- ☑ I've learnt that the only time you will be an expert on parenting is when you don't have any.
- ☑ Gay people are not necessarily happy.
- ☑ Having a cat is not like having a child, it's like having a cat.
- ☑ Asleep is the new awake.
- ☑ That even when I text message I have to use capital letters and punctuation marks, otherwise the world will collapse.
- ☑ That I love the approach of winter so I can say finally say goodbye to all that disagreeable sunshine.
- ☑ That even therapists (perhaps especially therapists) need love and approval.
- ☑ If you want to change your child's behaviour then you have to change your own first.
- ☑ That my children have done a perfectly inadequate job of raising me.
- ☑ That in order to hold onto your children you have to let them go.
- ☑ Never take your mobile phone out to lunch with you. That way if something happens, you are uncontactable.
- ☑ That my high school yearbook quote, 'If at first you don't succeed – give up', has finally morphed into, 'If at first you don't give up – you will succeed.'